Total Home Makeover

Renee Metzler

RENEW YOUR SPACE & SPIRIT

Total Home Makeover

Renee Metzler

20
day planner

AMBASSADOR INTERNATIONAL
GREENVILLE, SOUTH CAROLINA & BELFAST, NORTHERN IRELAND

www.ambassador-international.com

Total Home Makeover
A 20-Day Plan to Renew Your Space and Spirit

Printed in the United States of America

ISBN: 978-1-62020-013-1
eISBN: 978-1-62020-055-1

Cover Art by Kaysha Siemens
Book Design and Page Layout by Matthew Mulder

AMBASSADOR INTERNATIONAL
Emerald House
427 Wade Hampton Blvd.
Greenville, SC 29609, USA
www.ambassador-international.com

AMBASSADOR BOOKS
The Mount
2 Woodstock Link
Belfast, BT6 8DD, Northern Ireland, UK
www.ambassador-international.com

The colophon is a trademark of Ambassador

To my Heavenly Father

Thank you for your favor, outrageous plans, presence, and love.

To Nevin

I'm so blessed to have you as my husband, best friend, cheer leader, and soul mate. Thank you for always believing in me. I love and appreciate you for all that you are. After over ten years of marriage, I am still "in like."

To Daphne

My dear daughter, I love who you are. I appreciate your leadership qualities, your gifts of speech and art, your fun nature, and just watching you create and imagine. You bring so much joy into my life. I love your presence, and I'm proud to call you my daughter.

To Chloe

I love your soft, gentle spirit and your sense of humor, my dear daughter. Thank you for being someone who cares about others. I appreciate your gifts of tenderness and peacemaking and how beautifully creative you are. I love being with you, and I'm proud to call you my daughter.

Contents

Phase Three

Acknowledgments

EVERY GOOD GIFT COMES FROM above, and so I give God the glory for any great idea within these pages. I also want to thank my husband, Nevin, and daughters, Daphne and Chloe, for encouraging me to press on and finish my book. Embracing my love for writing required me to close my "home business" doors and step out in faith to open a new chapter in my life, pursuing the concept of "Total Home Makeover." Thank you, my dear family, for nudging me in the right direction. You've taught me that it's always worth pursuing our dreams, risking failure (though it really can't hurt or stop us), and going on the walk that requires faith.

Creating a book is a team process, and so I want to recognize those who have helped:

- ☼ All of the wonderful people at Ambassador International, for believing in my manuscript. Thank you for applying your expertise in editing, design, marketing, and publishing. Thank you for the highly professional and godly manner in which your company works and for taking my manuscript from rough draft to book-shelf worthy. I am truly grateful for the experience of developing this project with you.

- ☼ Dr. Samuel Lowry, for believing in and acquiring my manuscript

✹ Tim Lowry, for over-seeing the project with excellence

✹ Matthew Mulder, for his creative design and direction

✹ Brenda Covert, for her friendly editing expertise

✹ Alison Storm, for her marketing expertise

✹ Shannon, my sister-in-law, for kindly sharing home organizational ideas and tips, some of which I have incorporated into this book.

✹ Cheri, for giving me reader feedback; that perspective is invaluable.

✹ Dad and Mom, for praying for the success of this project and for the general support I have felt.

✹ All the friends and family in my life who have encouraged me, and to Marti Statler, for being first to "fall in love" with my manuscript.

✹ Trina, my photographer, for the author picture; you are truly gifted.

A Prayer

Dear Father in Heaven,

Thank you for being the giver of all life, all order and beauty, all creativity, all wisdom, all gifts, and all good ideas. I praise you for placing this book in the hands of your beautiful child. I believe this twenty-day plan includes practical keys to living well in the natural. I realize that you have created us with body, mind, and soul. Your gift of practical living is just as much from you as your gifts of spiritual life. I ask for a special endowment of grace, strength, energy, creativity, joy, and problem-solving for this reader, your dear daughter, as she reads and applies this twenty-day plan.

I also ask that you would guide her every day as she completes this journey from chaos to order in her home. Help her to absorb the concepts, adopt healthy home habits, and see this twenty-day plan to completion. Rally those around her to support her, and place the right support partner(s) in her path.

We ask that your will for beauty, order, and *life* come on earth as it is in heaven.

Thank you for being a supernatural God who can do more than we've ever asked or imagined. I love you, Abba Father.

I pray this in Jesus' name,
Renee Metzler, your follower

WELCOME TO
Total Home Makeover

I'M RENEE METZLER, AND I am proud to coach you on a subject that can help everyone who dwells in a home: effective home management. I'm also a follower of Jesus, freelance writer, wife, mother, and life management coach through my site at Http://totalhomemakeover.com and blog at Http://reneejoyjourney.com .

Back in 2002, I found myself in a strange predicament, one that I hope you will never have to experience. I began a brand new career for which I had not trained—as "home manager." As I struggled through the first couple of weeks in my new "position," I found myself facing an ugly truth. I was lacking in home management skills, knowledge, and discipline. My performance was a C+ at best. You see, I had trained to become a secondary education English teacher, but I had never really trained to manage a home well. I say well, because many of us can manage somewhat, but well is another story.

When I was pregnant with my first child, I decided to make that drastic career change. I went from full-time teacher to full-time mother and home manager. I didn't buy into the world's theory that you're only important if you have a big paycheck, a big home, lots of stuff, and a high status career. However, I am a believer in doing well in that which we seek out to do. I knew that, as the hours of my day flew by without much structure, I had a few things to learn about how to manage a home. I noticed that some women seemed to struggle like I did, and then others seemed to keep their homes in order without much effort. Thus began my quest for the secrets to smarter home management.

I began to ask questions, read books, and look for information online. Were there tricks to the trade of home management? Did successful home managers have "secrets" or a common ground of knowledge and skills that we floundering ones lacked? Did great home management mean I would never have time to pursue my other dreams? Was home management out of style, or did people still desire a safe place where family is valued, where tears are okay, where dinner and a hug are waiting, where we can unwind and rest in a peaceful environment?

It's been nine years of research, practice, and writing, but I'm happy to report that the answer is … emphatically, yes! There really are secrets to the trade. There really are systems that work better than others. There still is a human need for a haven called home. I applied my findings to my own home, and I found that these secrets to the trade of home management work and are worth passing on to others.

I'm still not a perfect homemaker, but that was never my goal. My goal was to find systems that make homemaking more effortless, so I can focus on doing the other things in life I love. I guess I want the best of both worlds. I want to pursue my dreams and still enjoy coming home to a fairly orderly house! I'm proud to share these ideas with you. If you are someone who longs to come home to more order than chaos, but you want your order through less effort, then this book is for you.

Who is this book for?

- ✵ **Young and Old** – If you are young and are just starting to learn how to manage a home, this book will help you get off to a great start. You will learn order-producing habits for life. If you consider yourself old, it is a great time to improve upon your years of experience. You may find that some of the routines that I teach will help bring even more order into your life and free up your time.

- ✵ **Career Woman and the Full-time Home Manager** – There are certain tasks that simply need to be done every day and every week to keep a home running smoothly. Whether you spend many hours at home or only a few, you will still want an efficient system that takes less time. You can benefit from applying faster and smarter routines to your home. More hours at home doesn't always equal a more orderly home. However, smarter routines and healthy habits do.

- ✵ **Mothers** – As parents, we need to model successful living skills. Life skills are learned in the home. Children learn more from what we do than what we say. Showing your children how to manage well is the best way to pass on a legacy of successful living. No matter what stage your children are at, there are still certain things that must be done every day and every week to bring order to your home. If these things are neglected, such as washing dishes, your home will move toward chaos quickly. Adjust the routines to fit your schedule, but do fit them into your day. Children are not an excuse to live in chaos, but rather they are the reason to model excellence.

✿ **The Perfectionist or the Scattered** – You may be a perfectionist and spend all your hours cleaning and organizing but really long to spend more time with others. The routines and systems in this book can help you to stay on task of what really needs done and then free yourself to do the other things you love. If you tend to be scattered and lost without structure, I'm supplying you with the structure you will need so that you can enjoy the home environment around you.

What You Get

Total Home Makeover is a twenty-day plan to making simple, positive changes to your life that will take you from chaos to order. Won't you agree that as a woman, you long to come home to an orderly home? And yet, most likely you don't want to spend hours upon hours making your home orderly. Like many women, you may long to arrive at point B (an orderly home), but you are currently at point A (a chaotic home). You wish to arrive at your new destination, but the journey is unclear and seems too long. Be encouraged, because in this twenty-day book, I will take your hand and guide you, step-by-step, toward a destination of order. The plan in Total Home Makeover will help you arrive at point B—an orderly home—in just twenty days. During your journey, you will complete three Phases of Order. During this twenty-day journey, you will get yourself, your family, and your home all rowing in the same direction, toward order. When you do, something will click, and home management will become more effortless. It will be like rowing a boat down a stream.

Phase 1 – Transform You. Learn personal healthy habits through the use of daily and weekly routines. We all live by our habits. Most likely, you have a morning routine. You get up, get ready, and get out the door. When you are completing this morning routine, do you leave behind a trail of trash, mess, and dirty clothes? If your honest answer was yes, then phase 1 will help you to re-create habits that bring order. This will transform your home. Perhaps you aren't leaving behind a trail of trash and mess but would like to add a few smart steps to your routine so that your home order takes less effort. In phase 1, I'll teach you to create and use successful daily and weekly routines. These routines will help you develop personal habits that produce order in your home for a lifetime.

Phase 2 – Transform your Family. Properly train and praise your family to develop healthy home habits. Once you have taken responsibility for your own personal habits and are using smart daily and weekly routines, you are ready to get the family to move toward order. If you are the only family member bringing order, and the rest of the family is moving toward chaos, who do you think will win? You're right, chaos will win. We can't have that! Phase 2 is very important. I'll teach you how to coach and train your family to help around the home. I'll also show you how to choose a specific chore time, how to track their success, and how to offer rewards to keep them motivated. Once the whole family is moving toward order, your goal of home order will become more effortless.

Phase 3 – Transform your Home. It's time to organize your home to fit your family's lifestyle. Now that you personally have learned order-producing habits and your family is helping to bring order, you are ready for phase 3, room-by-room organization. I purposely saved phase 3 for last because I knew you would be frustrated if you organized your entire home, only to have your family or yourself sabotage your hard work.

Now that you are each working toward having healthy home habits, it's time to organize each room. In phase 3, I'll teach you a simple three-step organization technique. First, you'll design your space into activity zones that meet the needs of your family's lifestyle. Then, you'll clear, sort, and containerize. We'll apply this same simple technique to every room. At the end of this phase, your unwanted items will be purged, your useful items will be stored in their own container, and you will be able to breathe again (not to mention find the remote).

Get Started

At the beginning of every phase, I'll give you an overview of what to expect in that phase. You'll want to read this carefully before you begin your new phase to make sure you have everything you need to accomplish that week's challenge.

You'll begin your journey at Day One! Each day you can expect the following:

Daily Renewal – Think of Daily Renewal as eating a PB&J "spiritual" sandwich. Just like our bodies, our spirits need to be fed. P stands for Prayer, B stands for Bible Reading and J stands for Journaling. Each morning, it's so important to take a few moments to feed your spirit. Your daily PB&J spiritual sandwich will keep your spirit nourished for the journey.

Let's Chat – This is your personal ten-minute coaching session. Think of me as your coach, someone who's been there (in home chaos). Grab a cup of coffee, and let's chat each day about one "bite-sized" topic. For example, on day one, we'll talk about developing a daily routine that brings order. I'll show you my sample daily routine and discuss important key elements. At the end of the "Let's Chat" section, you will be equipped to create your own daily routine. This session is designed to help you improve one day and one topic at a time.

Get Moving – This is your daily to do list. Reading about change doesn't bring change. It's only when we "get moving" and apply what we just learned that we will begin to see the transformation toward order in our lives. On day one, during our "Let's Chat," we'll discuss daily routines. Then, I'll hand you your daily "get moving" list, and you will create and complete your daily routine. The Get Moving List applies what you just learned in our chat session for that day.

Personal anecdotes – As your coach, I want you to know that I'm just like you, someone trying to improve and grow in home management. I'll share some of the stories from my journey just to make you smile.

Joy Tools – These are ideas to bring joy into the task of home management. We might as well "whistle while we work."

Work Sheets – You can use the interactive work sheets to help you on your journey. The work sheets are designed to help you accomplish your daily "Get Moving" list such as "Design my Space" and the "Planning Calendar."

Rewards – At the end of each week, I encourage you to celebrate your success by picking a reward from my treasure trousseau. You can enjoy your reward alone or with a friend. Going on a life-changing journey requires stopping and celebrating. The rewards are designed to keep you motivated.

"THE HOMEMAKER HAS THE ULTIMATE CAREER. ALL OTHER CAREERS EXIST FOR ONE PURPOSE ONLY—AND THAT IS TO SUPPORT THE ULTIMATE CAREER."   ~ C.S. LEWIS

You're Not Alone

AND, YOU WON'T BE ALONE. You'll have a personal coach, a partner, and a website. No one wants to go on a journey alone. Here are the traveling companions that I recommend for the journey.

- ☼ **Personal Coach**. That's Me! I've been where you are, and I'm excited to share keys to home management in your personal daily coaching session, called Coffee Chat. You can also ask questions by e-mailing me at Renee@totalhomemakeover.com or commenting at Http://totalhomemakeover.com.

- ☼ **Choose a Partner**. You can journey alone, but I recommend choosing a partner. You can invite a sister, best friend, daughter, or even a small group to join in the fun. By partnering, you'll be most likely to achieve success because you'll gain accountability, focus, and encouragement.

- ☼ My Partner(s): _____.
  Start Date: _____.

- ☼ **Supportive Website**: Http://totalhomemakeover.com Get more ideas, share your thoughts in the Coffee Chat

Forum, get updates on my journey, schedule a Life Makeover Workshop, join the Victory Club.

A journey consists of going from point A to point B. This book will direct you from chaos to order in your home. Imagine what your home will look like when you've arrived at your destination. Do you see harmony, peace, efficiency, and clarity? Just like any journey, you will experience challenges and bumps along the way. It will help to keep your eye on the prize: an orderly and functional home. If you commit to keep moving forward, you will reach your destination. Don't stop until you've arrived at point B. If it takes you longer than twenty days, it's okay. As long as you keep moving forward, you will arrive.

You can do it!

Renee - Friend, Coach, and Fellow Mom

PHASE ONE
Transform Yourself

> I AM THANKFUL FOR A LAWN THAT NEEDS MOWING, WINDOWS THAT NEED CLEANING AND GUTTERS THAT NEED FIXING BECAUSE IT MEANS I HAVE A HOME.... I AM THANKFUL FOR THE PILES OF LAUNDRY AND IRONING BECAUSE IT MEANS MY LOVED ONES ARE NEARBY.
>
> ~ NANCIE J. CARMODY

ARE YOU EXCITED FOR YOUR journey? Imagine yourself in a row boat. You are in the front. In the far distance, there is a beautiful town called Order. The very first thing you must do to reach that town is to begin rowing. Behind you is the town called Chaos. The crime rate is high, and the streets are dirty. You have two other people in your boat, "Family" and "Home." You need to get all three rowing toward order, but as the coach, you have to begin rowing first. In Phase One, you will transform yourself. Then you will be able to lead both your family and your home to your destination: order. I can't wait to see you arrive!

Here is what you can expect in phase one. Phase one is all about creating personal healthy habits or routines that result in an orderly home. These routines changed my life, and I know they will change yours too. Here's what you'll do each day this week.

Day 1 – Create a successful Daily Routine. I'll show you what needs to be done each day to create order in the home. We'll put these key components into a smart daily routine that saves time and steps. You can customize the daily routine to fit your lifestyle. The daily routine is the number one secret to home management success.

Day 2 – Create a Weekly Routine that brings order. Just like your daily routine, there are certain home tasks that need to be done one time each week. If you tackle one task each day, you'll have a manageable weekly routine. Once you have your routines in place, it will feel like your home is on autopilot. Without a weekly routine, you might think things like: *"I'm overwhelmed. It's Saturday. I want to have fun with the family, but I have piles of laundry to do."* In contrast, with a weekly routine, you might think: *"I feel in control of my home. Each day, I complete one task, and I know on Saturday my home will be in order so I can play with the family."* A smart weekly routine is the number two secret to home management success.

Day 3 – Learn some meal planning strategies. Now that you have a daily and weekly routine in place, I will begin to teach some of the key elements of those routines in more detail. For example, part of my weekly routine is "Monday Meal planning." Meal planning is essential for great home management because it will save you time and money. I'll share my secrets to successful meal planning.

Day 4 – Basics of desk work, errands, and laundry. These tasks make up part of your weekly routine. I'll take one day to share tips and explain the process of managing each task well. Desk work will lead to better financial success. Errands will help to keep your home stocked in essentials. Laundry day will help to keep your family clothed. That's pretty important. **Day 5 – Planning 101.** Planning is a key element to successful home management. There are many family activities to juggle, and having a plan for your life is important for being proactive. Being proactive means you are in "the know." You are prepared for your week and the events that will take place, such as hair appointments and your child's school play.

Planning will help you feel more in control of your daily life. It will help you avoid those "panic" moments such as, "*I completely forgot about my sister's birthday party!*" Instead, you'll always be prepared.

Get excited! Phase one will bring you instant success in just five short days. I once read that habits determine almost ninety percent of what we do. In Phase One, we are retraining your daily and weekly habits with patterns of success. Anyone can learn to be a great home manager. You can develop personal healthy habits that bring order, and these routines will be your road map. You may wish to be extra-prepared by reading the lists below.

Tool Box

Read over the list below and consider having these items or tools on hand for the upcoming week. They will assist you in completing this week's goals.

- ☼ **Kitchen Timer.** Use this to time yourself when completing tasks. You can accomplish the same task in less time by setting a time goal. (optional)
- ☼ **Date Book.** Use this for weekly planning.
- ☼ **Highlighters** in yellow, blue, green, pink, orange, purple. We'll use these for planning on Day 5.

Renee's Favorite Resources

Extra resources to learn more on this week's topics

Websites

Http://totalhomemakeover.com for success stories, free resources, and support

www.flylady.net for more ideas on daily routines

www.thehomeschoolmom.com for free printable planners for daily routines

www.organizedhome.com for free printable planners

www.keepandshare.com for a free on-line calendar

DAILY RENEWAL

ARE YOU READY TO GET renewed and eat your first PB&J "spiritual" sandwich? Feeding your spirit is essential for maintaining strength on your life journey. Remember, P stands for prayer, B stands for Bible, and J stands for journaling. Before digging into our coaching session, take a moment to renew your spirit.

A Word about Prayer: Our communication with God is called prayer. Communication is two-way. We communicate with our spouse by both listening (receiving a message) and talking (sending a message). God wants to both listen and talk to you. The entire Bible records God speaking and listening to His people. This is recorded in both the Old and New Testaments. The Bible is His written Word and is our checking point because His written Word will always back up what He is saying today.

You've heard the saying, "It's about a relationship, not a religion." I want to challenge you to know God as intimately as you know your best friend or spouse. Ask Him questions and wait for His answer. Consider journaling your questions and the answers that you receive. Just as He communicated in the Bible (through dreams, visions, a burning bush, a still, small voice, an appearance on the road to Damascus, through a prophet friend, etc.), God still speaks today, and he is speaking to you. *Aren't you excited?* The living God, your Heavenly Dad, loves you and longs for you to know Him as well as He knows you. You really aren't alone. When He speaks (in the form He chooses), your answer may be, "Yes, Lord, your daughter is listening."

Bible: *The Lord is God, and He has made His light shine on us. . . Give thanks to the Lord, for He is good. His love endures forever* (Psalm 118:27, 29).

Prayer: Dad in heaven, thank you for shining your light on me and through me. Thank you that you notice me and love me for all eternity. Thank you that you think I'm amazing just being me, not based on how well I perform. You delight in me, and I want to know and delight in you. What is on your heart today? Your daughter is listening. (I recommend journaling your two-way communication with Him in the journal portion below. Write what is on your heart.)

Journal:

_____

_____

_____

_____

_____

_____

_____

_____

_____

_____

LET'S CHAT... ABOUT DAILY ROUTINES!

I'm so excited to get your home into fabulous condition! The first secret to great home management is smart daily routines. Daily routines are the things you do each day. These things can either bring chaos or order. For example, each morning you get up, get ready, and get going for the day. This is your morning routine. During this morning routine, you can choose to leave behind a trail of mess, or you can play it smart and do little things to bring order as you go. Adding little things that bring order as you go will diminish your work load later.

Reactive. When it comes to home management, most people are in reactive mode. They are constantly reacting to the mess (their own messes) and trying to catch up. If there is a pile of dishes, it's time to do dishes, which means supper will be late. If the clothes are all dirty, it's time to do laundry, which means there might be frustration in the morning trying to get dressed with a minimally clean wardrobe. Reactive mode can be stressful.

Proactive. Then there are those few home managers who always seem to have their homes in order. The clutter is managed, the dishes are done, and the clothes are clean. These people are proactive. They seem to be on top of the mess before it even happens. After researching[1] and asking questions, I realized these proactive home managers know a secret.

The secret is smart daily routines. These simple routines are like a road map to blissful home order. There are certain tasks that must be done every day to keep your home running smoothly. When you put these tasks into a smart daily routine, you can avoid the frustrations of reactive home management, and you will enjoy the environment of an orderly home. Here are the seven daily tasks:

The Seven Daily Tasks

- ☼ make your bed
- ☼ deal with obvious dirt (such as wiping dirty counters or sweeping a dirty kitchen floor as needed)
- ☼ attack laundry (complete one load a day to avoid the pile up)
- ☼ prepare meals
- ☼ wash the dishes and shine sink, counters, and stove
- ☼ attend to mail, papers, and phone calls
- ☼ hit the hot spots (A hot spot is where clutter gathers. It needs to find a home!)

Get Determined Mentally. As you look around your house, you might feel overwhelmed. You might think, *How can I find the time to complete a daily routine? How can I add something else to my overwhelming schedule?* Let me assure you that when you complete your daily routine consistently, you will gain control of the chaos in your home and ultimately gain more time. Get determined about making healthy changes in your life. Choose to think positively. Say, "I will become a proactive home manager. I can do this."

You will reach your destination, order, if you choose to keep a positive perspective. In Victoria Osteen's book, *Love Your Life*, she shares a story about mind-sets.

"I heard a story about a little girl who whined and complained about everything one day. The next day she was cheerful and sweet to everyone. Her mother said, 'Yesterday, you had such a bad attitude. Today, you're happy about everything. What happened?' The little girl replied, 'Yesterday my thoughts were pushing me around. Today I'm pushing my thoughts around.'"[2]

It's time to get determined mentally. It's time to break old habits and push our thoughts where we want them to go. It's time to get proactive about home management. I can't wait for you to encounter the difference, in just one day, when you complete your daily routine.

Let's put these seven tasks into a daily morning and evening routine. Notice how the flow of my sample daily routine saves you time and steps. No back-tracking. The daily routine is like putting your home on auto-pilot. It is the number one key to successful home management. This routine will be your guide or your road map to maintaining order for a lifetime.

Renee's Sample Daily Routine
Morning Routine

1. **Me**. Get up and make bed. Go to the bathroom and get gorgeous. Deal with obvious dirt. You can simply swipe with a wipe to leave the bathroom clean.

2. **My House.** Take dirty clothes to laundry room and attack laundry. Start a load! Go to kitchen. Get out a clean dish cloth and tea towel for the day. Empty the dishwasher. Now, think dinner. Crock pot? Thaw meat? Then, think breakfast. Feed your family and pets. Remember any vitamins and medications! Enjoy a three-minute family devotion, prayer, and review of today's schedule. Have EVERYONE clear the table and "feed" the dishwasher.

3. **My Mental Check.** Before heading out the door, check your calendar for appointments and review daily to-do

list. Any time left? Use "little minutes" to clear a hot spot, such as putting away shoes that are cluttering your entryway.

Evening Routine

1. **My Family.** Start by filling your sink with hot, soapy water. Prepare dinner. Soak and wash as you go for less clean-up later. After dinner, EVERYONE helps to clear the table and "feed the dishwasher." Prepare for tomorrow. Do you need to pack lunches? Get coffee ready. Wipe down counters and sink. While you have the family together, enlist their help in a quick tidy. Play "tidy ten" with young children and count to ten as you put away items. You can give a reward such as a sticker on a chart.

2. **My Chores.** Attack your laundry. Dry, fold, and put away! Don't leave it in the basket! Also, sort through mail and school papers, complete paperwork, and return phone calls. Deal with any obvious dirt such as sweeping the kitchen floor and hit a hot spot by putting away clutter for even one minute!

3. **My Plan.** It's important to plan for tomorrow. Write down your most important things to do for tomorrow. Make one your top priority. This will focus you for the next day.

GET MOVING!

✓ Customize your morning and evening routine to fit your lifestyle. Try to include the seven daily tasks. Analyze for efficiency. Write it down and post it on your fridge.

Adjust as needed or as your life changes. Note: You will complete the weekly routine tomorrow.

✓ Complete your morning and evening routine today (and from now on).

Joy Tool: If you have children, a bedtime routine is essential for them. I begin this routine at 8 pm. If my girls are hungry, they get a bedtime snack. Next, they get a bath and brush their teeth. Then, Daddy or I sit in bed with them and read to them. We often read from the Bible, a Bible story book, or a devotional at their level. Recently, we've been reading a children's devotional book that guides children to seek God and His kingdom. We've begun to seek God together, which has helped to open up a whole new spiritual level to our relationship. We then end our bedtime routine with a prayer to God and a time to cuddle, talk, and connect.

Joy Tools: Bringing joy to your daily routine is important. We can "whistle while we work," to quote Snow White. I hope that by now you are convinced that a daily routine for your home is essential. I would like to compare it to your personal daily hygiene. Just as taking a shower and brushing your teeth are key elements for good personal hygiene, so the daily routine is essential to your home hygiene. It's important to do these little things to make your home run smoothly. Isn't it true that people like to be around you when you don't smell? Isn't your home more enjoyable to be around when it is maintained well? Since I know we both agree that daily hygiene of the home is important, I want to challenge you to ask the following question: *"How can I bring more joy to my daily routine?"* Sometimes the piles of work seem so overwhelming that we would rather run in the opposite direction. Trust me, I know. I can be the master of procrastination. However, when I do my daily routine, I feel free to focus more on accomplishing the other things I love! Here are a few suggestions for bringing joy to your daily routine.

1. Play music that inspires you or draws you closer to God during your morning routine.

2. Reward yourself when it's finished by enjoying a few moments of your favorite morning show, communicating via e-mail or face book, or getting introspective with your journal and coffee.

3. Prayer. Why not include praying for your family as you unload the dish washer in the morning before they leave to face the world for the day?

Simple Daily Routine

Morning

1. Make bed
2. Primp & tidy bathroom
3. Attack laundry
4. Kitchen: empty dishwasher, prepare for dinner, breakfast
5. Clean-up breakfast
6. Review to-do list
7. Hot Spot Minute
8. Out the door with a smile

Evening

1. Return to a tidy home
2. Prepare dinner and eat
3. Clean dishes and shine sink
4. Tidy-up home, hitting the hot spots
5. Attack laundry again
6. Mail, papers, phone calls
7. Obvious dirt and daily chore
8. Clean litter box
9. Take out the trash (Mondays)
10. Me time!

My Smart Routines
My Weekly Routine

MON: _____

TUES: _____

WED: _____

THURS: _____

FRI: _____

My Morning Routine

1. _____
2. _____
3. _____
4. _____
5. _____
6. _____
7. _____
8. _____
9. _____
10. _____

My Evening Routine

1. _____
2. _____
3. _____
4. _____
5. _____
6. _____
7. _____
8. _____
9. _____
10. _____

DAILY RENEWAL

Bible: *But those who hope in the LORD will renew their strength. They will soar on wings like eagles; they will run and not grow weary, they will walk and not be faint* (Isaiah 40:31, NIV).

Prayer: Dad in Heaven, thanks for equipping me with everything I need for today, including strength to form habits of success in my home management. My hope is in you today. Fill me with your strength so I soar, run, and walk. What would you have me learn today? Your daughter is listening.

Journal:

_____

_____

_____

_____

_____

_____

_____

_____

_____

_____

LET'S CHAT... ABOUT WEEKLY ROUTINES

Congrats! Yesterday, you created and completed your daily routine. This will give you order daily. Before we have today's coaching session, you should have already accomplished your daily routine. Isn't it amazing how it transforms your home? Be proud of your success, because you are building new, healthy home habits.

Today, we'll focus on creating a weekly routine. The weekly routine is more about the major home tasks that need to be done each week. I'll break those tasks into five categories. We'll call them your Charming Chores. You can tackle one Charming Chore each day. The weekly routine will give you even more control of your home. Then, the weekends are for play.

A weekly routine has been an age-old secret to home management. Our pioneer mothers knew that maintaining their homes through a weekly routine meant survival. When I was a child, my dad read a favorite book series to me by Laura Ingalls Wilder. In *Little House in the Big Woods*, Laura shares her pioneer mother's weekly home management routine.

"Each day had its own proper work. Ma used to say:

"Wash on Monday,
Iron on Tuesday,
Mend on Wednesday,
Churn on Thursday,
Clean on Friday,
Bake on Saturday,
Rest on Sunday." [3]

The weekly routine consists of completing one C̲h̲a̲r̲m̲i̲n̲g̲
Chore each week day. When you tackle each day's "proper work,"
you'll become a proactive home manager. You'll be ahead of
your game. Here is the order I prefer, but you can customize
the weekly routine to fit your schedule. Also, be aware that your
family can help with these chores too. We'll talk about family
involvement a little later.

Five Charming Chores

- ☼ **Meal Plan Monday**. Create a meal plan that is cost
  effective, delicious and nutritious, and takes less time.
  Create a grocery list. **Tip!** Keep a list on your fridge for
  jotting down depleted supplies. For free meal plan ideas,
  go to my blog, http://renee-joyjourney.com.

- ☼ **Desk Work Tuesday.** It's a good idea to write bills,
  send thank you notes, file, and balance your check book
  before you go shopping for the week.

- ☼ **Errands on Wednesday**. This can include a trip to the
  grocery store, post office, bank, dry cleaners, and library.
  Compiling your errands into one day saves time and
  gas.

- ☼ **Laundry on Thursday.** Even though the daily routine
  reminds us to stay on top of laundry each day, the reality
  is you'll need a day to focus on catching up completely.
  Plus, don't neglect the wrinkly pile.

- ☼ **Wave Clean Friday.** Unless you live alone, most homes
  need a basic cleaning weekly. Get out the cleaning caddy,
  turn up the music, and speed clean your home in two
  hours, or hire someone else to do it!

Bonus! Don't forget to take out the trash on garbage truck day!

Keep it simple. Do one chore each day. Keep it logical. You obviously want a meal plan, grocery list, and a balanced check book before errand day. But do customize the five tasks to fit your life.

GET MOVING!

✓ Grab your pencil and plan your weekly routine on the Routine Worksheet. Post on fridge.

✓ Complete today's Charming Chore (as listed on your weekly routine).

✓ Complete your morning and evening routine.

Sample Weekly Routine

Daily Charming Chores
Meal Plan Monday
Desk Work Tuesday
Errands Wednesday
Laundry Thursday
Wave Clean Friday
Remember Trash Day

Joy Tool: How can you bring more life and joy into your weekly routine? My sister-in-law, Shannon, enjoys praying and mowing at the same time. I enjoy listening to spiritual teaching, talking to God, or listening to worship music when I'm running errands. I also enjoy getting my cleaning done quickly so I can move on to other things. When I clean, I set a timer to help me remain focused and efficient. Look inward and ask yourself, "What would bring me more joy and life as I do my weekly routine?" Write your ideas here.

_____

_____

_____

_____

_____

_____

_____

_____

_____

_____

_____

_____

_____

_____

_____

_____

Joy Tool: Managing a home does take effort and strength, even when using smarter routines. I love to set my alarm clock a few minutes early. I often will use those extra minutes to hit the snooze button so I can spend a few minutes resting in God's presence. That is one way I am filled with His strength for the day.

DAILY RENEWAL

Bible: *"It has been written, Man shall not live and be upheld and sustained by bread alone, but by every word that comes forth from the mouth of God"* (Matthew 4:4, AMP).

Prayer: Dad in Heaven, thank you for giving me both physical and spiritual life. As I learn to plan meals, help me to be a wise steward of your "bread." I recognize that both your bread and every word that comes from your mouth uphold and sustain me. I am truly grateful. What words are you speaking to me today? Your daughter is listening.

Journal:

_____

_____

_____

_____

_____

_____

_____

_____

LET'S CHAT... ABOUT MEAL PLANNING

Bravo! You've reached Day 3 of your Total Home Makeover Challenge. Before we begin our chat, please remember to be consistent and build your healthy home habits. Complete your morning routine and daily charming chore if you haven't already. Then, we can begin our session.

Today, let's chat about meal planning. Meal planning is part of my weekly routine, and I usually complete this on Mondays. Planning "what's for dinner" plus breakfast, lunch, and snack ideas is important for your family's nutrition and for your budget. Did you know that when you plan your meals, you tend to spend less at the grocery store? Today, I'll show you how I do it. To get started, let's consider four criteria to consider when planning meals:

The Bottom Line. A bottom line is the amount of money you choose to spend on groceries. By choosing a bottom line, such as $35, $50, or $100, you gain control of your grocery spending. Once you have a spending goal, your mind will work to find solutions to meet that goal.

Many people believe the lie that they are not in control of the grocery budget. They complain about rising grocery prices and how much they spend at the stores, but they aren't willing to choose a bottom line and stick to it. I decided to take my bottom line theory to the limits. I made a goal to feed my family on $35 a week. Could it be done? Once I made the goal, I looked for ways to meet that goal.

☼   First, I chose healthy meals that were cost effective, such as tuna cakes, meatloaf, and soups. I call these $5 dinner solutions.

✿ Then, I shopped at a deep discount store. I know of other women who look for sales at multiple stores and also clip coupons, but I didn't have the patience to do that. So, I chose a store that offered deep discounts on everything. I also find savings at my local farmers' market.

Guess what? I really can feed my family on $35 a week. Do I always stick to this goal? No, sometimes I spend $50 or even a little more. I just like knowing that I can control how much I spend. Making a bottom line spending goal will give you control of your spending. Then your mind will look for ways to meet that goal. To view a detailed sample of a $35 weekly meal plan, go to my blog at http://Renee-joyjourney.com.

Drive a Hard Bargain. When my husband and I were first married, we decided to go on a cruise. We had an amazing time encountering other islands and other cultures. One of our stops was Jamaica. At Jamaica, we had the chance to walk through a market lined with vendors and all kinds of "goods." We had an opportunity to purchase a souvenir.

A beautiful necklace caught my eye. The seller must have noticed, because before I could ask about the price, he spoke up and offered it for twenty dollars. I wasn't used to such aggressive selling. So, my reaction was to back away. I told him I would think about it. He immediately came back with a counteroffer and said I could have it for fifteen dollars. I said that I'd think about it and walked away. We got about twenty feet away, and a man came running with the necklace and said he would give it to me for just ten. "Really?" I thought. I placed the necklace around my neck and paid the man ten dollars in cash. I had made a "hard bargain" without even trying.

You can make a hard bargain with your grocery budget too. Don't just accept expensive prices. Don't let retailers decide how much you will spend. Create a bottom line spending goal and find a way to stick to it. If your regular grocery store's prices are too high, go to a local farmers market or a deep discount shopping store. Stores like Aldi and Save-a-lot offer forty to fifty percent off normal grocery store prices. Remember, you are in control of your grocery budget.

Delicious. Make sure you and your family love the taste of the meals you are preparing. This is the "yum" factor. Experiment with different food genres and begin to record a list of your family's favorites. I like to have plenty of resources to pull from, such as cookbooks, a recipe box, food magazines, and websites. **Tip!** Plain meals can be made "gourmet" with the right seasonings.

Nutritious.★ Most experts agree that a balanced diet is the way to go.★ You may wish to follow these five healthy guidelines for nutrition. 1) Choose five servings of fruits and veggies daily; 2) choose two servings of milk daily; 3) include protein rich foods; 4) limit alcohol, sugars, and high fats; and 5) drink six glasses of water daily.

Making sure your family is getting the array of necessary nutrition during meal time is a top priority for meal planning. Also, consider avoiding processed foods. Stay as close to nature as possible.

No Time at All. Many women feel busy today. For the busy cook, saving time in your cooking might mean using smarter and quicker techniques. Here are my top five favorite fast techniques!

1. Make a double batch and then either freeze or have left-overs. You gain a free night of no cooking!
2. Use quick and easy recipes and fast ingredients. Get a cookbook that offers this.

3. Use quick tools such as your crock pot and di

4. Have emergency favorites such as an omelet or quesadillas with salsa.

5. Keep a frozen pizza on hand at all times! Add a salad, and voilà!

As I walk you through meal planning, think "bottom line, nutritious, delicious, and no time at all." Now, let's begin!

Three Steps to Budget Meal Planning

✿ **First, gather your supplies.** You'll need a pen, a meal planning worksheet, and recipes. You may also wish to have a three-ring binder or purchase a notebook to collect your weekly meal plans so you can reuse them next year. I write mine in a simple notebook! As you select recipes, remember to write down the page numbers for easy reference. **Tip!** Print a free weekly meal planning sheet online at http://renee-joyjourney.blogspot.com/2011/01/meal-plan-monday.html

✿ **Choose your menu for the week.** First, decide "what's for dinner" (five to seven dinners). I like to plan in variety. I might choose a double batch of soup, a chicken dinner, ground beef dinner, vegetarian dinner (bean or egg), and fish or pork dinner. Remember to cook according to seasons, for instance, corn on the cob in the summer! Save time by planning for the freezer. Whip up a double batch of lasagna. And remember to use your crock pot. I like to make soup weekly for easy lunches. I also plan only five dinners per week to allow for leftovers and eating out. After you've decided "what's for dinner," then choose simple BLS ideas (breakfast, lunch, and snack). Try to work vegetables, fruits, and nuts into the BLS plan for added nutrition. For healthy snack ideas, include yogurt, popcorn, pretzels, fresh fruits and vegetable, and nuts.

☼ **Create your Bottom Line and Grocery List.** Based on your recipes, now it's time to make a grocery list. I highly recommend starting with a bottom line. That is, first decide how much you want to spend, and then create your meal plan and grocery list. You may have to clip coupons or go to a discount grocery store to reach your bottom line goal, but you will feel in control of your grocery budget when you do this. To avoid feelings of "failure," select an attainable goal to begin.

Tip! Super busy women may wish to use a meal planning source such as my $35 Weekly Meal Plan at my blog (Http:// Renee-joyjourney.com) or another favorite source.

★ Please consult with your doctor for a diet plan that is right for you.

GET MOVING!

✓ Complete your morning and evening routines.

✓ Complete your menu plan and grocery list for this week.

✓ Complete your Charming Chore.

From my Life

Focus. I've wanted to write this book since 2002. I started it, but then I also started a new business. Although I learned a lot through this great experience, I felt that God was saying, "Close this door, and I will open a better door." Even though it was difficult to let go of the familiar, I obeyed. My heart wasn't in the past, but I had to step out in faith for the future. What I really wanted to do was complete this book. I heard it once said that you can't chase two rabbits at one time. What dreams do you really want to pursue? Sometimes we have to eliminate a rabbit. We need to focus on our most important dream. When we remain focused on just one dream, we are more likely to achieve what we set out to do.

Joy Tool: Women love to help others. Personally, I've gained great amounts of joy through helping other women with practical ideas through my blog. Do you have a great $5 dinner solution? In other words, do you have a favorite family meal that is very cost effective? You can help other women by sharing your $5 dinner solution (and recipe) at my blog (Http://Renee-joyjourney.com). Also, feel free to get great $5 dinner ideas there from other women like you.

Menu Planner

My Bottom Line: $ _____

(Remember to write down recipe page numbers.)

What's for Dinner?

Monday _____

Tuesday _____

Wednesday _____

Thursday _____

Friday _____

Saturday & Sunday _____

Dessert

_____

B L S (Breakfast, Lunch, and Snack Ideas)

_____

_____

_____

_____

Grocery List

Produce	Canned/ Packaged	Dairy
_____	_____	_____
_____	_____	_____
_____	_____	_____
_____	_____	_____
_____	_____	_____
_____	_____	_____
_____	_____	_____
_____	_____	_____
_____	_____	_____
_____	_____	_____
_____	_____	_____
_____	_____	_____
_____	_____	_____
_____	_____	_____
_____	_____	_____
_____	_____	_____
_____	_____	_____
_____	_____	_____
_____	_____	_____
_____	_____	_____

Grocery List

Meats	Freezer	Other

DAILY RENEWAL

Bible: *Jesus gave them this answer: "I tell you the truth, the Son can do nothing by himself; he can do only what he sees his Father doing, because whatever the Father does the Son also does. For the Father loves the Son and shows him all he does"* (John 5:19-20, NIV).

Prayer: Dad in heaven, I surrender my day and life to you. Please reveal to me what you are doing so that I may enter into *your* work. I recognize that there is value in taking care of my earthly home but that it must never come above my relationship with you. What is on your heart today? Your daughter is listening.

Journal:

_____

_____

_____

_____

_____

_____

_____

_____

LET'S CHAT... ABOUT DESK WORK, ERRANDS, AND LAUNDRY

You are doing great! You are reprogramming yourself to complete successful daily and weekly routines. Are you noticing the improvements in your home? Soon, your daily routines will be a habit. Now, let's chat more about your weekly routine.

Remember, there are five "charming chores" that make up your weekly routine. It's much easier to tackle only one charming chore each day. For example, I told you that Mondays are my meal planning days. In today's Coffee Chat, I'd like to describe, in more detail, three more charming chores. These include desk work, errands, and laundry. If you are willing to tackle one charming chore per week day, your great reward is that your home will not go to chaos by the weekend. Your bills will be paid, your clothes will be clean when you need them, and your errands will already be accomplished.

This is a proactive approach to home management. It will bring order to your home and free up your weekends to spend more time with family and friends. The benefits of a proactive lifestyle are obvious. Let's take a brief look at the following three charming chores.

Desk work needs to be attacked weekly. Whether your home office is a file accordion, a tucked away desk, or a whole room complete with office furniture, here is a list of the basic tasks that need to be done each week to stay on top of your desk work.

✿ **Sort mail** – I recommend first throwing out all junk mail. Then, deal with your bills. I file bills in the order they are due in a visible location at my desk. Near the stamp area of the envelope, I write down the due date so that I can easily see which bills need to be paid. Finally, you may want to file keepsake notes in a file box or place letters of correspondence in a nearby organizer bin.

❋ **Pay bills** – I'm sure you know how to do this task. Make checks and pay bills that are due. You can pay online with many companies. However, I still like to receive that paper bill in the mail so that I'm more aware of my upcoming expenses. When you write a check, you realize how much you are actually dishing out to heating companies, phone companies, etc.

❋ **Record and file receipts** – Record your receipts from last week and balance your check book. This is important to avoid overcharge fees.

❋ **Review your budget** – Take a look at your monthly budget and make sure you are on track.

❋ **Return correspondence** – Do you need to RSVP for upcoming birthday parties, write thank you notes, send a birthday card, answer e-mails, or return a phone call? Desk day is a great day to complete this task.

Errands. Wednesday is often my errand day. It's a good idea to complete your errands all on one day because it will save you both time and fuel money. Before you go on your errands, make a list of needed errands and put them in a logical driving order. Make sure you have everything you need before leaving, such as your grocery list, mail, library books, and banking. Have you ever gone on errands and forgot a needed item such as your dry cleaning? It's very frustrating. Making your list and taking the time to gather those items will save you that frustration.

TIP! If you get easily bored driving, you could add interest to your driving time by listening to educational or inspirational CDs.

Laundry and Ironing. Laundry attacked every day is not so overwhelming on Laundry Day. However, with a family of three or more, you may find that a load a day just isn't enough. The benefit to keeping up with laundry is pretty evident. As children get older, teach them to be responsible for putting away their own clothes and eventually caring for their clothes from start to finish—a skill they'll need for life. The basic flow of your laundry process goes like this:

- ☼ **Gather**. Go through the entire house and get dirty laundry from hampers in each room.
- ☼ **Sort**. Sort clothes into piles of whites, lights, darks, jeans, delicates, and towels.
- ☼ **Wash**. Stain-treat with a spray-and-wash product. Use fabric softener.
- ☼ **Dry**. Dry on-line or in dryer.
- ☼ **Fold**. Fold as soon as dryer cycle is done to prevent wrinkles. Hang up as much as possible.
- ☼ **Iron**. If needed, iron.
- ☼ **Put away**. Don't neglect the last but MOST IMPORTANT STEP! Everything needs a home.

GET MOVING!

- ✓ Complete morning and evening routines.
- ✓ Complete today's Charming Chore.

DAILY RENEWAL

Bible: *Going a little farther, [Jesus] fell with his face to the ground and prayed, "My Father, if it is possible, may this cup be taken from me. Yet not as I will, but as you will"* (Matthew 26:39, NIV).

Prayer: Dad in heaven, as I learn to plan my weeks effectively, please make my spirit sensitive to your will. Help me to hold my plans loosely and be surrendered to your perfect plans, just like Jesus. What is on your heart today? Your daughter is listening.

Journal:

_____

_____

_____

_____

_____

_____

_____

_____

_____

_____

_____

LET'S CHAT... ABOUT WEEKLY PLANNING

Today, let's chat about weekly planning. Planning is a topic I adore. I believe it's essential for living a balanced life. Planning is a powerful tool for designing your life, living in balance, and living proactively rather than in a "last minute" crisis mode. You already have a daily and weekly routine planned. Just follow that home management plan, and it will be like running your home on auto pilot.

However, there are other aspects to your life outside of home management that you must keep in balance, such as time with God, family, and yourself. Planning helps you decide where you want your time to go. Try to be sensitive to where God is leading you. Nothing is more exciting than planning with God. Be open and surrendered to His guidance in your life as you plan. Let His plan become your plan.

Plan your Week. Here is a simple yet extremely effective way to plan your week. I like to sit down on Sunday nights and take a few moments to look at my week-at-a-glance date book and plan according to the values I hold dear. For example, my first value is to nurture my relationship with God. So, I block off time to seek God's presence and hear from Him. In other words, I set aside time to pray, read the Bible, and journal what I receive from my heavenly Dad (Deut. 6:5). Then, I plan in time for my other priorities, such as family, career, and self.

Time management experts recommend color coding your date book based on the different priorities. For example, you might color code a God time block yellow. This allows you to step back and see that you are matching your time with your priorities. Here are the different priorities I schedule into my week and the order in which I plan. You may wish to highlight each priority in a different color.

Plan According to Priorities.

☼ **God**. (time to renew spiritually and mentally through Bible study, praise, journaling, and communicating with God) -Yellow

☼ **Family**. (includes special time with husband, children, and family activities) -Blue

☼ **Home**. (the care and management of the home) -Orange

☼ **Work**. (your career or job) -Green

☼ **Self**. (emotional & physical health, enjoyments, self-care) -Purple

☼ **Relationships with Friends & Extended Family**. -Pink

☼ **Appointments** & Working on **Personal Goals**. -Black Ink

Now, let's grab your weekly planner and highlighters. Begin with planning next week according to your top priorities. Do you want to begin by scheduling in time to seek God? If so, block off time with God and highlight those blocks in yellow.

Highlight time blocks. As you plan in your time, highlight your time slots with the correlating color. This will let you see visually if you are living a balanced life. For example, if there is minimal purple (Self) or blue (Family), but lots of green (Job), you may be overworking yourself. Ask yourself, "Is money really worth missing out on rich relationships with my family and friends?" Make necessary changes to live a more balanced life that you desire. Also, remember to schedule in appointments and time for your personal goals. I recommend color coding for a month until you have designed a balanced week that you are truly happy with and that works for your family as well.

Embrace God Appointments. Don't be surprised when God throws in an adventure or a God appointment. It's a "good thing" to throw your plan out the door in order to embrace God's greater plan. God didn't tell us not to plan or not to be purposeful about our lives. But He did tell us to seek Him first and His kingdom so that we don't miss out on the good things He has in store for us. I can attest to this.

God's Plans Are Greater. I worked hard for four years building my own sales business, but I believed God wanted me to finish this book. When I finally stopped kicking around in the dirt with my own plans and started stepping out in faith with the dreams God had placed in my heart, the doors flung wide open. God poured out His favor on me. He gave me the opportunity to publish this book. Now, instead of struggling to succeed in one business, I get to do what I love every day. I get to write and create to bless others and glorify God. His plans really are to prosper us. *"For I know the plans I have for you,"* declares the LORD, *"plans to prosper you and not to harm you, plans to give you hope and a future"* (Jeremiah 29:11, NIV). He is an awesome God.

Remain Flexible. It's important to plan and to live our lives on purpose. However, we must also remain flexible. When our plans don't go the way we wanted, we can adjust ourselves or even laugh at our new situation.

My mother-in-law, Carol, loves gardening. Each year, the garden club to which she belongs hosts a bus trip to see a spectacular garden in our region. She has often invited me to go along. I looked forward to these trips with much anticipation. In my mind, the plan was to get dressed for a special day of touring, shopping. and talking. It would be the perfect "girls' day out."

However, things never went as planned. One year, my mother-in-law came back from the bus's bathroom and told me she couldn't find the light switch. I had to use the bathroom next. When I closed the small bathroom door, the bathroom had very little light. I groped around in the dark, looking for a light switch. I soon gave up. As I used the restroom, another lady came and opened up the door. Embarrassed, she quickly closed it. "Oh my goodness," I thought, "I forgot to lock the door." I reached up, slid the lock closed, and "there was light."

If I said that this embarrassing blunder was the worst of my mistakes during these trips, I would be lying. Each year, it never failed. An embarrassing moment took place. The perfect plan for a perfect day had a glitch. It became so habitual that I began to expect it.

One year, we had just arrived at our destination. The ladies all stopped to use the public restroom. We were all milling around outside waiting for everyone to gather. Carol and I were having a conversation when a teenage girl from our group came up behind me. She gently touched my shoulder and said, "*You have a piece of toilet paper hanging from your pants.*"

Our plans don't always go as planned, but if we remain flexible, we can still enjoy each day. I can laugh at these situations and not take myself so seriously. I am guessing that God likes to put little glitches in our plans. Wouldn't it be boring if everything was perfect? Glitches and embarrassing moments grow us and bring humor to our story. Remember to live on purpose and plan for a balanced life, but remain flexible at the same time.

GET MOVING!

✓ Plan the rest of this week and the upcoming week, using your favorite color coding method.

✓ Complete your morning and evening routines.

✓ Complete your daily Charming Chore!

✓ Check in with your partner today and share your successes on my website at http://totalhomemakeover.com

My Weekly Plan

Time	Monday	Tuesday	Wednesday	Thursday	Friday
5:00 AM					
6:00 AM					
7:00 AM					
8:00 AM					
9:00 AM					
10:00 AM					
11:00 AM					
NOON					
1:00 PM					
2:00 PM					
3:00 PM					
4:00 PM					
5:00 PM					
6:00 PM					
7:00 PM					
8:00 PM					
9:00 PM					
10:00 PM					

Saturday _____

Sunday _____

Renee's Sample Plan

Time	Monday	Tuesday	Wednesday	Thursday	Friday
5:00 AM					
6:00 AM					
7:00 AM	AM Routine	-----	-----	-----	-----
8:00 AM	Children To School - Daily Renewal		-----	-----	
9:00 AM	Exercise	-----	-----	-----	-----
10:00 AM	Writing	-----	-----	-----	-----
11:00 AM					
NOON	LUNCH TIME	-----	-----	-----	-----
1:00 PM	Meal Plan	Desk Work	Errands	Laundry	Wave Clean
2:00 PM					
3:00 PM					
4:00 PM	Ballet	-----	-----	-----	-----
5:00 PM	Music	-----	-----	-----	Family Fun Night
6:00 PM	DINNER	-----	-----	-----	-----
7:00 PM					
8:00 PM	PM Routine	-----	-----	-----	-----
9:00 PM	Me Time ... such as reading or writing!		-----	-----	
10:00 PM					

YOUR FIRST REWARD

"When tasks are done
And lessons learned,
A gold dusting
You now have earned,
Take hither from the list below,
One reward
From my trousseau."

Treasure Trousseau

1. Shop! Purchase one desired new item.
2. Glamour! Soak your feet and paint your nails.
3. Pamper! Take a hot bath with candles and soft music in your home spa.
4. Renew! Take a walk by yourself, enjoy nature, and reflect.
5. Inspire! Enjoy the arts – museum, theatrical play or symphony.
6. Utopia! Chat in a fun place like a coffee shop with a good friend.

Joy Tools

Through this journey called life, I have learned some valuable lessons that have brought me more freedom. I want to pass a few lessons on to you.

Lesson 1: When I take a break, I'm a better mom. If you worked for an employer 24/7, do you think you would be effective or moody? Is there any difference for the career of motherhood? "Mom's time out" is so important. You need time to refuel, reflect, know yourself, and refresh.

Lesson 2: I can retrain my mind to agree with God that I do have what it takes to accomplish my dreams. There was a time in my life when I was struggling with self-doubt. Let me point out that self-doubt is not from the Lord. During this time, I wasn't sure if I could accomplish the things I set out to do. To combat this, I spoke affirmations aloud daily for six months. I said things like:

☼ I have what it takes to accomplish my destiny.

☼ I am a child of God.

☼ His favor is chasing me down.

God tells us to renew our minds, and when we speak (especially out loud) and declare the truth about how God sees us and what God says about us, we can melt down lies of self-doubt and fear. We can replace those lies with the truth. After consistently retraining my mind with affirmations, I began to agree with God and believe how He felt about me. Then, a funny thing happened.

Once I began to believe, I was able to accomplish the goal I set out to accomplish. If you have self-doubt or fear, take courage. You can overcome! You don't have to stay in the same place you are right now. Don't doubt your ability to accomplish your dreams. That is a lie of the enemy. God placed both your dreams and the ability to accomplish those dreams inside of you. If you dream it, you can do it. But, you have to start by reminding yourself that you really can. Verbally affirm yourself out loud every day.

Lesson 3: I deserve rewards. When you do a great job, take time to reward yourself. You deserve a new outfit, a relaxing get-away, or a new book to stimulate your mind. You are worth it! Reward yourself.

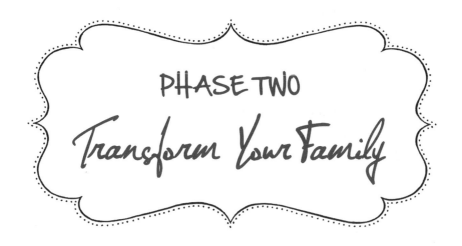

PHASE TWO

Transform Your Family

I LIKE HUGS AND I LIKE KISSES, BUT WHAT I REALLY LOVE IS HELP WITH THE DISHES!

~AUTHOR UNKNOWN

CONGRATULATIONS ON COMPLETING PHASE ONE of Total Home Makeover! I hope you enjoyed your reward. You earned it. You now have learned successful daily and weekly routines as well as Planning 101. You have transformed yourself to bring daily and weekly order.

Remember the row boat I described earlier? You are at the head, rowing toward a blissful town called Order. You're making some progress in this journey, but it's going to be a lot of hard rowing if the two people behind you row in the opposite direction.

In phase two, you will transform your family and get them rowing with you toward order as well. When everyone in the family is moving toward order, you can more quickly reach your goal. It's pretty easy. So, now it's time to focus on establishing yourself as a coach to your family. You can think of your family as a team that needs to learn how to work together. Plus, this week I'll teach you the simple process of room-by-room organization. Here's what you'll do this week.

☼ **Day 6** - Establish "you as coach," discuss family expectations, and track your family's progress with a reward chart.

☼ **Day 7** - Family Training part 2 with One-on-One Training. You'll get to explain and model the techniques of accomplishing a chore well.

☼ **Day 8** - Wave Cleaning. Today I'll teach you my favorite smart method of cleaning house. The family can easily participate with this method.

☼ **Day 9** - Organizing 101. I'll show you a simple, three-step method to organizing any space. Today, I'll teach you the process, and then we can get ready to begin Phase 3.

☼ **Day 10** - Phase 3 begins with room-by-room organizing. Let's start with the porch and foyer. You'll get to apply my simple, three-step organization processes to your porch and foyer area.

I can't wait to begin this week's challenges. You've probably already noticed a huge difference in your home by following the daily and weekly routines, but now you can get your home to run even more efficiently by training your family to move toward order as well. Here is a list of items you may need to accomplish this week's tasks.

Tool Box

☼ Paper for Reward Chart – This chart will be used to track your family's chore participation in the home and to remind them of the reward they will earn.

☼ Stickers for Reward Chart (stars)

☼ Cleaning Tote (optional) – It's easier to have all your cleaning products in one tote that can easily be carried from room to room.

☼ Two Trash Bags – You'll need two trash bags every time you set out to organize any space. One will be used for items that need to be tossed and the other for items that can be donated.

☼ Two Labels (optional) – You can write *donate* and *trash* on each label and place them on your two different trash bags. This will keep you from confusion as you place unwanted items in the trash bags when organizing.

Resources
Websites
Http://Renee-joyjourney.com for ideas, encouragement, support, and comments

www.chorechart.com for free printable chore chart

www.dltk-cards.com/chart for free printable customizable chore chart

DAILY RENEWAL

Bible: *Trust in the LORD with **all your heart** and lean not on your own understanding; in all your ways submit to him, and he will make your paths straight* (Proverbs 3:5-6, NIV).

Prayer: Dad in heaven, Thank you that I can trust you. I give you all areas of my heart. I place my family (and any other area of concern) into your capable hands. As I learn to parent well, please guide me and make my paths straight. What do you have to teach me today? Your daughter is listening.

Journal:

_____

_____

_____

_____

_____

_____

_____

_____

_____

_____

LET'S CHAT... ABOUT "YOU AS COACH & FAMILY EXPECTATIONS"

Welcome to phase two, transforming your family. You are moving right along, and let me be the first to congratulate you on developing personal home routines that bring order. Most likely, you are not the only one who lives in your house. Now, it's time to get your family on board.

Family is for helping. God gave us families so that we have a loving place to practice "doing life." When you invite your children into the process of "daily home chores," you are giving them the gift of hands-on learning.

One year just before Christmas, I invited my two young daughters, Daphne and Chloe, to make gingerbread cookies with me. My girls were delighted. We all put on our aprons and began our "hands-on learning." At first, things felt under control, but soon flour, sugar, and cookie cutters were strewn everywhere in my kitchen. I started to panic. I wanted to get strict. Instead, I took a deep breath and told myself, "Renee, let it go. You'll clean this up afterwards. Enjoy this hands-on learning experience with your girls." And then I did. Now, when my girls grow up, they too will have the all-important skill of gingerbread cookie making to share with their families.

Get Your Family on Board. Are you ready to get your family rowing toward order? If you have children, your home is a training ground for them. The Bible says to "train up a child in the way he should go" (Proverbs 22:6 NKJV). Children are in our homes for a short time. Now is the time to both model and train your child to create healthy home habits. Let's transform your family.

When it comes to guiding the family on home habits, I've tried different roles that simply did not work. Can you identify with my mistakes?

- ☼ **Servant**. "Here, kids, I'll pick up after your messes, get you all your drinks, and generally be your slave."

- ☼ **Drill Sergeant**. "That's it. I'm now blowing my stack. It is clean up time. Pick up your mess now! I'm cracking the whip."

- ☼ **Empty Threats or Bribes**. "Children, if you don't clean up your room, I'm not taking you to McDonalds." "Children, if you clean up your room, I'll take you to McDonalds."

Frankly, I've tried all three, and they don't work well. But, I will tell you what does work. In a firm but gentle and loving spirit, coach your family. Why? Coaches explain the game, demonstrate and model how to succeed at the game, have their team practice, track the team's progress, and give rewards to the team for a job well done. Proverbs 15:4a (NLT) says "Gentle words are a tree of life." Remember to use a gentle yet firm coaching approach to training your family to participate in home management. This will bring life to your family as you build healthy home habits together.

Begin with a Talk. Choose a time today when your entire family is together, such as dinner time, to discuss the following list. Let your family know beforehand that there will be a family meeting with some important and exciting news. At the meeting, discuss in a firm, positive manner the following:

- ☼ **Calmly explain the game.** "I know we all love when the home is in order. Don't you love it when you can find your shoes in the morning? I have learned successful routines to keep our home in order and am working at changing my habits for the better. And since we all live here, it is important that we all have great "home habits" so that we can all enjoy a pleasant home. Also, I want you to know how to live when you are grown. Let's pretend that I'm your coach, and we are all on the same team. Our goal is to have a pleasant and orderly home."

✿ **Show them their daily "to-do" list.** Note: Create "To-Do List" in advance. Show them their chore list. Be positive and excited. You can say, "Here are a few simple things I am asking you to do each day. Every day, right after dinner, it will be chore time. When you complete your to-do list, you will receive a star on your chart. When you've accumulated twenty stars on your chart, you win this month's game, and you will receive a prize we both agree on." Talk about each chore item. Choose rewards you both agree on, such as bowling night or a desired toy. Sign your names on the chore chart to finalize the agreement.

✿ **Demonstrate & Practice.** Tell them, "Today will be our first day. I will be showing you exactly how to do your list, and you will be practicing and learning. We will begin this right after dinner tonight and every week night." Then, demonstrate as needed and monitor their work. This will show them you care about how well the job is done. Praise their efforts as they go. Stay calm and firm. Try to keep chore time fairly short. For toddlers, it might be for only five to ten minutes. Older children can complete thirty to sixty minutes of work.

✿ **Track Daily.** Give out stars after the daily chore time to track their success. Verbally praise them!

☼ **Reward.** When the end of the month comes and they've reached twenty stars, give them their promised reward. Remember to praise them daily. This is like a gold dusting. It will keep them motivated. Make a new chart for the next month, choose a new reward, and begin again.

Can you imagine how much easier home life will become when all members are moving toward order? Having a daily chore time is building in the structure you'll need to keep children accountable for their home habits. This helps you with home management now, but it also trains your child to be neat for a lifetime. This can improve the lives of your children, grandchildren, great grandchildren, and beyond.

GET MOVING!

✓ Complete your morning and evening routines.

✓ Complete your daily Charming Chore.

✓ Create a Team To-Do Chart.

✓ Complete steps 1 through 5 above with your team today.

Joy Tools

Ideas on Tracking Chores for Your Family – Here are just two ideas you can use to track chores for your family. You are limited only by your imagination. Make chore tracking interesting, fun, and educational. Through earning rewards or money, children can learn how our world works and how to manage their money well.

☼ **Pretty Paper Pockets** – When my daughter was eight years old, she requested a job to earn money. So, I created two paper pockets labeled with each child's name, and I posted them on the fridge. Every day at chore time, I hand each daughter two or three index cards. On the index card, I've listed a chore with a money reward such as a quarter. For example, it might say, "Put Laundry Away for 25 cents." When they complete the chore, they can put the card into their paper pocket. They like how grown up it feels to earn their pay on Fridays.

✿ **A Game Board Chore Chart** – During the summer, I like to create a chore chart that looks like a game board similar to Chutes and Ladders. Each square has a chore; some are even fun activities. As the kids complete each chore, they put an **X** on the square. They win a toy or special gift when they complete the "game."

Submit your Ideas

Do you have a unique way of tracking children's chores? Send your ideas to nrmetzler@windstream.net and your ideas could be published at Http://totalhomemakeover. com or Renee's Blog at Http://Renee-joyjourney.com . Thanks for sharing with other moms and readers.

Chore Chart

Child's Name _____

My Chores

1. _____
2. _____
3. _____
4. _____
5. _____

My Progress

1 _____	6 _____	11 _____	16 _____
2 _____	7 _____	12 _____	17 _____
3 _____	8 _____	13 _____	18 _____
4 _____	9 _____	14 _____	19 _____
5 _____	10 _____	15 _____	20 _____

When I win twenty stars, my reward will be: _____

_____.

Signed by Child: _____

Signed by Parent: _____

Healthy Home Habits for Children

1. Make bed and put dirty clothes in the hamper.

2. If you make a mess, clean it up.

3. One thing at a time. Put your current toy/project away before getting out the next.

4. As soon as you walk in the door, put your things away in their homes (coats hung, shoes on rack, keys hung, book bag in closet, etc.).

5. Do your chores every day right after dinner (or designated time).

6. When finished eating, ask to be excused and take your dishes to the sink or dishwasher.

7. Respect other people's things and be kind. Remember your manners (please and thank you).

Sample Chores

Child Age 5-9

1. Make Bed
2. Feed and Water Pet
3. Carry Dirty Laundry to Hamper
4. Put Toys Away
5. Carry Dirty Dishes to Sink

Child Ages 10+

1. Shine Bathroom Sink
2. Wash Dishes
3. Put Laundry Away
4. Help Cook Dinner
5. Vacuum

DAILY RENEWAL

Bible: *Jesus told his disciples, "But when He, the Spirit of truth, comes, He will guide you into all the truth; for He will not speak on His own initiative, but whatever He hears, He will speak; and He will disclose to you what is to come"* (John 16:13).

Prayer: Dad in heaven, Thank you that your Holy Spirit is within me. I invite you to guide me with your truth today. Fill me with your wisdom and love. May it spill out into my parenting choices. Just as you guide me, may I also guide my children with your help. What would you have me learn today? Your daughter is listening.

Journal:

_____

_____

_____

_____

_____

_____

_____

_____

LET'S CHAT... ABOUT ONE-ON-ONE TRAINING

Good morning! Want to know a secret? People learn best by watching and doing. When it comes to teaching your children how to properly complete a chore, you'll get better results when you:

☼ Explain the skill.

☼ Model how to do the skill.

☼ Watch them practice the skill.

Explain. Model. Practice. When you do all three, you show them that you care that the job is done right. Remember that being positive and offering praise will help to keep your team pumped and motivated.

One-on-one Training. Today, we will reinforce good family habits through one-on-one training. You will explain, model, and have your child practice each chore for which they are responsible. You can't expect your team to complete the drills well if they haven't been properly coached. Using this training technique of explaining, modeling, and then practicing will thoroughly teach your children the skill or chore. You will also be sending them an underlying message that you care that the job is well done and you believe they are worth the time and training.

Have a Second Discussion. I also encourage you to have a second conversation about "healthy home habits" at the dinner table to reinforce what you discussed previously. Today, do the following:

☼ At dinner, remind your family of their chore chart and that they will begin right after dinner. Show them their charts and praise them on their star accomplishments so far. Remind them of their reward. Tell them that today, you will show them how to do their skill well (i.e., model making the bed neatly or sorting laundry). Tell them that you know they have what it takes to be excellent in their chores.

✿ In addition, discuss the following "Healthy Home Habits." Praise them for what they are doing, and encourage them to improve on the ones they are lacking.

Healthy Home Habits

✿ Each morning, make your bed and put dirty clothes in the hamper.

✿ If you make a mess, clean it up.

✿ One thing at a time. Put your current toy/project away before getting out the next.

✿ As soon as you walk in the door, put your things away in their homes (coats hung, shoes on rack, keys hung, book bag in closet, etc.).

✿ Do your share. Complete your chores every day right after dinner (or designated time).

✿ When finished eating, ask to be excused and take your dishes to the sink or dishwasher.

✿ Respect other people's things and be kind.

GET MOVING!

✓ Complete your morning and evening routines.

✓ Complete your daily Charming Chore!

✓ Dinner Chat as discussed above with lots of praise!

✓ One-on-One training with your team! Model the skills!

DAILY RENEWAL

Bible: *From that time on Jesus began to preach, "Repent, for the kingdom of heaven is near"* (Matthew 4:17, NIV).

Prayer: Dad in heaven, Thank you that your kingdom is near me. Thank you that I am your temple and that I carry your light and goodness. Fill my home and bless those who enter in through my door. Allow me to see and understand your kingdom more. What is on your heart today? Your daughter is listening.

Journal:

_____

_____

_____

_____

_____

_____

_____

_____

_____

_____

_____

LET'S CHAT... ABOUT CLEANING 101

Getting the dirt out of your home weekly will add a little sparkle to your life. Cleaning is one of those charming chores that generally should be done weekly. I've designated Friday as my cleaning day or rather, hour. Now that your home is generally tidy due to your new routines and family involvement, cleaning doesn't have to take all day. I can have my home clean in one and a half to two hours. Today, I want to share with you my favorite efficient technique to clean house. First, we'll discuss having the right tools, and then I'll share my favorite method—wave cleaning.

The Right Tools. You only need a few simple tools to complete your cleaning tasks. Save money and don't get swept up with all the fancy gadgets and cleaning products out there.

- plastic caddy (filled with cleaning essentials)
- small bucket – for washing floors
- rags & paper towels
- vacuum, broom, dust pan, & mop – for floor clean-up
- toilet cleaner & brush
- dusting solution (lemon oil) & dusting rag
- all purpose solution (for cleaning almost everything else)
- scrubbing cleanser, such as Comet (for sinks and tub)
- glass cleaner

Wave Cleaning. I enjoy having a clean home, but I don't want it to take up my entire life. I asked myself, "Is there a smarter way to clean? Can I do the same job in less time?" I began to research cleaning strategies. In a book called *Speed*

Cleaning 101, Laura Dellutri introduced me to the wonderful world of wave cleaning.4

This is my favorite efficient method for cleaning my home. I can usually complete the task in less than two hours, and it's very easy to involve my family. Many professional cleaners use this method because it's effective and time efficient. Think of this method as ocean waves.

With the first wave, go through your home and collect all your dirty laundry. If you're team cleaning with your family, your children can go through the house at the same time and collect all the trash. The third wave will be to clean all the glass. Only clean visible dirt as you go. Give yourself a time goal that will remind you to move quickly. Remember, cleaning doesn't have to take all day. The next wave can be dusting all furniture that has visible dirt. You will quickly sweep through the home, dusting away the dirt. To involve the family, you can put one child in charge of cleaning all glass and another child in charge of dusting. In the meantime, you can begin vacuuming all the floors and have your husband clean the toilets. Can you see how this method is time efficient?

Order of Waves. My favorite order to wave clean is listed below with an estimated amount of time for each chore. It takes approximately one and a half hours to two hours to complete. So set your timer and begin a wave. Your home will look fresh and new in no time.

- ✿ Gather all dirty laundry – 5 minutes
- ✿ Gather all trash – 5 minutes
- ✿ Clean visible dirt on glass – 10 minutes
- ✿ Dust wood – 15 minutes
- ✿ Vacuum/sweep floors, including porch – 30 minutes
- ✿ Clean Toilets – 5 minutes

✿ Scrub Shower & Sinks – 15 minutes

✿ Mop Wood & Vinyl Floors – 10 minutes

Joy Tools: Here are a few ideas to bring joy and fun to the task of wave cleaning.

✿ Clean to your favorite music, or use that time to pray for your children, their schools, your town, region, and nation.

✿ If there is a lot of clutter sitting around, play a Tidy Twenty Game before cleaning. Quickly put away twenty things in each room for amazing results.

✿ Hire a professional or consider a "family clean" on Saturday mornings.

GET MOVING!

✓ Complete your morning and evening routines.

✓ Complete your daily Charming Chore.

✓ Remember to initiate your Family's To-Do Time.

✓ Gather your cleaning supplies into a neat little caddy (try out the wave method this week).

Day 9

DAILY RENEWAL

Bible: *"Nor do men put new wine into old wineskins; otherwise the wineskins burst, and the wine pours out, and the wineskins are ruined; but they put new wine into fresh wineskins, and both are preserved"* (Matthew 9:17, NIV).

Prayer: Dad in heaven, as I clean out the clutter in my home, I invite you to clean out the clutter in my heart. Please reveal to me what needs to go. Give me grace and comfort to admit and face the truth. Give me a "new wineskin" so that I may receive your new wine. What do you want to clean up in me today? Your daughter is listening.

Journal:

_____

_____

_____

_____

_____

_____

_____

_____

LET'S CHAT... ABOUT ORGANIZING 101

Today we will discuss the basics to organizing any space. Now that your home management systems are in place, you are ready to begin Phase Three, organize your home room by room. At the end of this process, each room will be functional, well designed, and clutter free. Get excited!

Before we talk about the process of organization, let's first look at a common myth about material goods. This myth may shed some insight as to why our homes became unorganized in the first place. If we can conquer this material myth with some myth busters, then we can have victory in staying organized for life.

"Things Bring Happiness" is a Myth. Many people believe that the newest gadget or that brand new pair of shoes will bring happiness. I would have never admitted that I believed this lie. However, when I went shopping, I proved I believed it. I would get caught up in a beautifully packaged item and think I just had to have it. These were unplanned shopping trips. Does this sound familiar? If so, perhaps, you too suffer from believing a lie that bringing home yet another chotchke will bring you joy. It is a myth to believe that things bring true joy and fulfillment.

✿ **Myth Buster 1: People are the treasure, and things are tools.** Healthy relationships with God and people will bring true happiness. Let's put material things into perspective. We are made for relationships and heart connections. However, having a dishwasher, a beautifully decorated home, and a well-organized wardrobe can serve to enhance our lives. Remember, things are tools, not treasures.

☼ **Myth Buster 2: Too much stuff leads to unhappy results.** Believing stuff can fulfill us has led to some unhappy results in our lives. In the past, I brought home newly-purchased items only to find that I really didn't love them after all. Many times they ended up in a yard sale or at the charity thrift store. I shudder at how many dollars I wasted on toys my children barely enjoyed. I've come to believe that if my children can't pick up their toys in fifteen minutes or less, I've given them too much. Too many things equal too much responsibility. The naked truth is that **too much stuff: a) creates chaos in our homes, b) steals valuable time, and c) wastes ridiculous amounts of money.**

☼ **Myth Buster 3: Less is more...manageable.** We are fortunate to have things to serve as tools such as a dishwasher, a stove, and a conversation area. A key to managing your materials is to live by new principles. Understand that things are tools, not happiness. Plan before you shop. Ask, "Does this item serve a functional purpose?" Remember that **less is more... manageable.** For those who have too much, consider this: if you eliminate fifty percent of the stuff in your home, then you'll eliminate fifty percent of your housework. Take it from me, when I de-cluttered my home, something just clicked, and my home became easier to maintain! Less really is more manageable.

☼ **Myth Buster 4: Learn to manage what you already have.** Materially, we need to grow up and stop buying more things. Instead of shopping, let's learn to manage well what we already have. If we live in chaos, it's a big red flag that we need to have less and learn to manage at that level. There is a certain joy and pride in managing well, maintaining, and being responsible stewards.

Organizing 101

Now, let's look at the simple process of organizing a room. When we go into a room, we're going to take control with three easy steps. At the end of the process, your new area will be functional, organized, and clutter free.

Step 1: Design your space. First, we want to look objectively at your current room or space and give it purpose. What activities do you want to take place in this room? The first step in designing your space is to **choose activity zones for your room**.

What function do you want this room to serve? How are you currently using this room? What activities do you want to be able to do in this room? Look at each room with fresh eyes. Perhaps you never dine in your dining room. What is the purpose of an empty dining room? There is no purpose. It is wasted space. Maybe you long for an art studio where you can have all your art supplies, put on the jazz music, and create beauty on a canvas. Do you see the obvious solution? You could easily turn your dining room into that art studio.

After you've chosen your room's activity zones, you'll then **draw a room layout** on graph paper. This doesn't have to be an exact scale. Just get your general pieces of furniture down and show where each activity zone will be located. For example, your buffet might serve as an art storing supply zone. Your dining room table might serve as your art project zone. Having a layout will give you vision for your current organizational project.

To design your space, first make a list of activities you and your family need and love to do, and then de-

cide where each activity zone will be on your layout. Get creative and think outside the box.

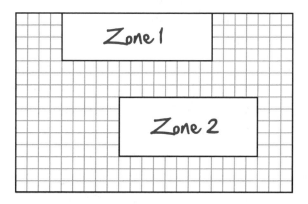

Design your Dining Room Sample

Zone 1

Zone 2

Zone 1: Art Supply Storage

Zone 2: Art Project Table

Step 2: Clear and sort the area

Now that you have decided on the purpose(s) of your room (activity zones) and have designed the space, you want to clear out what is already there. As you clear, you will sort into three piles: trash, give-away, and keep.

Trash Pile – Throw away items that are broken and have no value to anyone. Have a garbage bag handy to trash these items immediately.

Give-away Pile – Give-away items still have value, but you and your family no longer use them. Have a box or garbage bag handy that is labeled "give-away" to immediately place items in as you clear and sort an area. With give-away items, you can do the following to unload them.

✿ Donate – If you plan on donating unwanted goods, make a list of each item as you place it in your donation box so that you can count it as a tax write off. Don't put dirty, damaged, or broken items in the box.

✿ Yard sale – If you plan on hosting a yard sale, save a step and price items before storing (10% of the original cost is a typical yard sale price).

✿ Sell online – You could make a list of your inventory, take pictures, and post your unwanted goods on an on-line selling source such as craigslist.com or ebay.com.

Keep Pile. If an item is relevant to the room you are organizing, keep it. Pile like items together. For example, in your art supply zone, make one pile of paints, one pile of art paper, one pile of pencils, and one pile of paint containers. These will be your organized "keep piles." If you have a keep item, but it belongs in another room such as your bedroom, take it there or place in a box and take it there later. As you determine what to keep, ask the following question: **Have we used this item in the past year?** If yes, consider keeping. If no, get it out of there. You have to put on a professional hat and get stern with yourself when making these decisions.

Donated to Store: _____ Date: _____

Item   Estimated Value

_____   _____

_____   _____

Step 3: Containerize your keep items. Now that you have cleared and sorted the area, look at what keep piles you have sitting around. Take note of how large each pile is. Write down estimated sizes of containers you will need for each keep pile.

Try to problem solve. Do you have any containers already that would work to hold each pile? You might have a pretty basket that you can use to hold your paints. You might have a bench that would hold art projects and papers. You might use a decorated tin can to contain your art pencils. If you need to purchase containers, take your container list to the store so you can get the correct size. Remember, to containerize, choose appropriately-sized containers for your items and store like items together.

Choose my Containers

Keep Piles	Est. Size of Container	Solution/Budget
_____	_____	_____
_____	_____	_____

Wrap it up! To wrap up your organizing project, do a few more things. Place the trash items in the trash now! Get rid of it. Take care of the give-away items right away. If you are donating, deliver now or at least put it in the car and plan to drop off at your local donation store this week. If you are planning a yard sale, make sure everything is priced and put that box into storage now. If you are posting on Craigslist or eBay, post it right away and put the items in temporary storage. Decide to hold Craigslist items for only one month or less. After that, I recommend donating!

GET MOVING!

✓ Complete your morning and evening routines.

✓ Complete your daily Charming Chore!

✓ Remember to initiate your Family's To-Do Time!

✓ Prepare two trash bags (one labeled "trash" & the other labeled "donate" or "yard sale").

✓ Read Phase Three, Heads Up!

Learn the Lesson: Shop with a plan. When I began organizing my home, I took bags and bags of stuff to our local discount store. It was disheartening to think about all the wasted dollars. I know many of you will admit the same. There were toys that were almost new, clothes that didn't quite fit, household items that didn't match. Unplanned purchases and spontaneous shopping was the bottom line problem that I finally had to face. Shop with a plan and shop with your true needs in mind.

In the next phase, we will go into each room and apply this simple organizational process: design your space, clear and sort, and containerize. When phase three is complete, you will gain greater home efficiency and attain peace of mind.

IF YOU HAVE A CLUTTER PROBLEM, PERHAPS YOU HAVE BELIEVED THE LIE THAT THINGS ARE THE TREASURE. REPLACE THAT LIE WITH TRUTH. THINGS ARE A TOOL, AND PEOPLE ARE THE TREASURE! GET RID OF THAT EXTRA CLUTTER SO YOU DON'T SPEND YOUR TIME MANAGING THINGS BUT RATHER, SPEND YOUR TIME KNOWING YOUR LOVED ONES' HEARTS.

From my life. The reason I'm so passionate about the subject of life management is because I've really had to work at it. For example, I like to organize, yet I find I'm not always organized. What an oxymoron.

Take the shopping trip to the outlets that I once took with my mother-in-law. My daughter was probably two and a half at the time. I had grabbed the diaper bag but forgot to "reorganize" it—or even check for supplies, for that matter. Well, as luck would have it, I had one diaper and about two wipes left. We had begun our shopping fun, but it wasn't very long before my daughter's diaper was completely soaked. So I changed her into the last dry diaper, and I continued shopping.

My mother-in-law and I proceeded to go into an upscale store. I remember the clean appearance, the glass cases, and the stern looks of the clerks. My daughter was sitting on the floor as I browsed at some nearby merchandise. (In a store like that, it's not called "stuff," its called merchandise.) Anyway, I glanced over and noticed that my daughter was finger-painting on the crystal clear glass case. My breath caught in my throat. What on earth could her medium be?

She had gone "poo poo" and used that to paint her picture! We had to ask for paper towels, change her back into the wet diaper and, under our masked, muffled laughter, clean up the area. We headed off to a grocery store for more diapers.

What is the moral of the story? Never leave home unprepared! Of course, our mistakes can lead to great embarrassing moments that we can use to help other mothers feel better about their mistakes. I hope you feel like a master mother now.

PHASE THREE
Transform Your Home

DON'T AGONIZE. ORGANIZE.

~ FLORYNCE KENNEDY

CONGRATULATIONS ON COMPLETING PHASES ONE and two! So far, you've created daily and weekly routines, you've enrolled your family's help, and you've learned the simple process of organization. You should be so proud of all of your success. I know I am proud, and to prove it, after today's lesson, you'll receive your second reward.

In phase three, you will transform your home to work for you and not against you. You and your family are all rowing the boat toward your destination, Order. Now, it's time to get your home rowing toward order as well. To get your home in order, we'll apply a simple, three-step organizational process to each room. Our goal is to make each room clutter-free and purpose-oriented. Each room will have a clear purpose with activity zones, and each zone will have the "stuff" that belongs there.

If this phase takes you longer than expected, don't despair; just keep going. Understand that—depending on your level of chaos—you may want to take more time for each room than one day. If you work long hours at a job, you may need to continue completing your daily and weekly routines and make a goal to spend Saturday mornings working on organizing a particular room.

Reaching your Destination – Order. You can reach your destination. Obstacles such as busy schedules and defeated mindsets can make us want to quit. My daughter, Chloe, has requested to go to Disney World. Our family was hoping to go at a specific time; however, some obstacles stopped us. Does that mean we won't arrive at Disney World in the future? No. Keep on this journey toward order, and you will arrive. If you're very busy, give yourself extra time to complete the journey. Just like any trip, if you determine to keep going toward your destination; you will arrive. You can do it.

Here's what you'll do in Phase Three: Organizing Room by Room.

☼ Day 10 – Organize the Porch & Foyer

☼ Day 11 – Organize the Laundry Room

☼ Day 12 – Organize the Home Office

☼ Day 13 – Organize the Family Room

☼ Day 14 – Organize the Kitchen

☼ Day 15 – Organize the Dining Room

Reward!

☼ Day 16 – Organize the Master Bedroom

☼ Day 17 –Organize the Master Wardrobe

☼ Day 18 – Organize the Children's Bedroom

☼ Day 19 – Organize the Bathroom(s)

☼ Day 20 – Organize the Storage & Maintenance Plan

Final Gift & Applause!

You may wish to be extra-prepared for Phase Three by reading the lists below!

Shopping List - things you will need for Phase Three

- ✓ Containers to organize as needed
- ✓ Trash Bag labeled "throw out"
- ✓ Trash Bag labeled "donate" or "yard sale"
- ✓ Paper & Pen to list items you are donating (for taxes)

DAILY RENEWAL

Bible: *"Dwell in Me, and I will dwell in you. [Live in Me, and I will live in you.] Just as no branch can bear fruit of itself without abiding in (being vitally united to) the vine, neither can you bear fruit unless you **abide** in Me"* (John 15:4, AMP).

Prayer: Dad in heaven, I invite you to dwell in me, and I long to dwell in you. May your Holy Spirit fill me up with peace, hope, joy, and love. Thank you for your tangible presence. There is no life outside of you. I am thirsty for you, Lord. Fill me up and quench my thirst. Be alive in me that I might bear fruit. What is on your heart today? Your daughter is listening.

Journal:

_____

_____

_____

_____

_____

_____

_____

_____

LET'S CHAT... ABOUT ORGANIZING THE PORCH AND FOYER

Today we're going to organize the porch and foyer. I can hardly wait! You will apply the simple three-step process to organizing. For each room, you'll have a "Design your Space" worksheet to guide you through the process: design the space, clear and sort, and containerize. As you begin to objectively look at the porch and foyer, ask yourself what purpose or activities need to take place there. Some common activity zones could include:

☼ Welcome Zone (front porch or stoop)

☼ Conversation Zone (if you have room on a porch)

☼ Dining Zone (if you have room on a patio)

☼ Transition Zone (Foyer) – a place to take off shoes and coats and a place to store keys, purse, coats, hats, gloves, backpacks, and shoes.

Think about Smarter Routines. As you begin to design your space, think about your typical routines. You might enter the door, place book bags and coats on a hook, and drop shoes into a shoe cubby or basket. You also need to hang keys on a nearby hook and put mail into a mail inbox. As you think about smarter routines, ask yourself, "How can I save steps when laying out my activity zones?" Having a shoe cubby close to the hanging coats will save steps. Having a welcome mat by the door will help to keep dirt from being tracked into the house and save cleaning time later. Think about your routine and how you can save steps and time.

What to Keep. Here are some items you may wish to keep in your zones to create function. You may find that you have items that you really don't need. Get rid of them. You may find that you need items to complete an area. Buy them or put them on your shopping wish list. Take a look at what to keep.

Welcome Zone (Porch or Stoop)
☼ welcome mat
☼ seasonal wreath
☼ crock filled with seasonal plants

Conversation Zone (optional: if space is available)
☼ seating for typical group size

Foyer Zone (a place to transition into the home)
☼ hooks or pegs for hanging school bags and coats
☼ closet or coat rack for hanging all coats
☼ baskets or bins for shoes, purses, outerwear essentials such as hats and gloves
☼ hooks for keys
☼ mail-in/mail-out slots

GET MOVING!

✓ Complete your morning and evening routines.
✓ Complete your daily Charming Chore!
✓ Remember to initiate your Family's To-Do Time.
✓ Organize Porch.
✓ Organize Foyer.

✓ Check in with your partner and share your success and tips at http://renee-joyjourney.com under the "home" link.

✓ Receive your reward for completing ten days.

Design your Foyer

Step 1: Choose Activity Zones and Layout

_____

_____

_____

_____

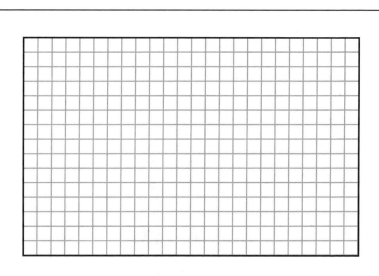

Step 2: Clear and Sort into 3 Piles (Trash, Give-away, or Keep)

Give-away Items	Est. Value	Give-away Items	Est. Value

Step 3: Choose Containers

Keep Piles (Like Items)	Est. Size	Container Solution (Budget)

YOUR SECOND REWARD

"You've coached the team
With praise and stars,
Your family wonders
Who you are,
You've turned into a dynamo,
Now take a treasure
From my trousseau!"

Treasure Trousseau

1. Treat! Treat yourself to your favorite dessert.
2. Glamour! Give yourself a makeover.
3. Pamper! Request a massage from hubby, drink herbal tea, & watch the stars.
4. Renew! Plan a day all to yourself. Do what you love.
5. Inspire! Enjoy the arts—poetry reading, a live band, a dance lesson.
6. Utopia! Go on a romantic date with your significant other.

From my Life

When I was young, I dreamed of many wondrous things. And now that I'm older, I dream of many more. What were your childhood dreams? If you're not careful, it's easy to lose your dreams. Don't lose yourself by trying to fit into a mold that isn't you. Don't let performance keep you from being original. It's easy to lose ourselves in this life. If you've experienced a disappointment, don't stop dreaming. Pick up where you are and keep moving forward.

The greatest gift you have to give to this world is to discover who you truly are and give it away. It's time to find you once again. What's in your heart? What are your desires? God will place the desires in your heart, so it's important to pay attention to what is there.

Do you love to write, as I do? Have you always longed to dance or sing or listen to people? What are your dreams? Start dreaming again. Write them down. Share them with someone who consistently encourages you. Take little steps toward your dreams. Allow the Author of dreams to open doors for you. You have what it takes to accomplish them.

One **of my dreams** is to help *free* people. Freedom is an attainable process. You can be free to be you. I believe there are different areas in our lives where we need to gain freedom.

1. **Free your spirit.** First, we must get spiritually free. We gain access to our Father through the blood of Jesus. We are filled with His Holy Spirit and now have access to the river of love when we seek His face. It's like being connected to a grapevine. Jesus is the vine.

2. **Free your mind.** Spiritual salvation is only the beginning. Next comes the renewing of the mind. You might be spiritually saved but still have all kinds of negative and

destructive lies and beliefs in your mind. If you chose to agree with the enemy rather than God, you can choose to melt down those thoughts and grow new, life-giving thoughts[5]. Read God's Word and agree with what He thinks about you. Jesus said that He didn't come to condemn. Do not condemn yourself. Speak positive truths. You do have what it takes to do what needs to be done. You do belong to your heavenly Father. Nothing can separate YOU from the love of God.

3. **Free your heart.** First of all, listen to your heart. It tells you many things. Stop denying your heart. Your heart is your "truth" checking point. Ask Jesus to heal your heart. Healing and forgiveness are a process.

Know who you are and your unique design. Knowing God, your Creator, will really help in understanding how He designed you. He didn't make a bunch of robots; He made dynamic, interesting individuals. You have a unique design, and life is your adventure. You get to discover your natural interests and gifts. He gave you the seeds, but you get to grow in your skills and develop and nurture your gifting. Listen to the dreams of your heart, look at your natural gifts, develop and discover.

1. **Share your gifts with the world.** Whatever your gift is, the world needs it. You have both spiritual and physical gifts that need to be discovered and shared. God designed us all as an intricate mosaic; each little piece is an important part to making our world an amazing place. Expressing your gifts will bring you great joy and fulfillment because you will be expressing who you were designed to be.

2. **Encourage others to develop their gifts.** Since we
   are all uniquely designed, there is no need for competi-
   tion. The adventure is developing ourselves and sharing
   the gifts we have. There is no pride, because every good
   and excellent thing is from above. No two gifts will look
   alike, because you are the only "you" on this planet. No
   two journeys will look alike, and any time is the right
   time to develop yourself. See another's gift, name it, and
   call it out. See your own gift, name it, and call it out.

God designed you and wants you to be passionate about developing and sharing your gifts with the world. Getting spiritually free is only the beginning. God didn't come just to free us
spiritually and then have us be miserable in our minds, hearts,
and physical life. Remember, He is the God who created the
Garden of Eden. He doesn't create misery! Jesus came to give
us **total** freedom.

Wherever you are right now, you are not stuck. Being in
the Father's presence daily will bring you strength, joy, peace,
and purpose for the journey. Get totally free and help free others. Free your spirit through the gift of Jesus' blood on the cross
and by connecting to our loving Heavenly Father. Free your
mind by renewing in God's truth daily and by speaking positive
truths about yourself. Free your heart through forgiveness and
allowing Jesus to heal you. Free your gifts by discovering and
developing your passion and your dreams.

DAILY RENEWAL

Bible: *"'In the last days, God says, I will pour out my Spirit on all people. Your sons and daughters will prophesy, your young men will see visions, your old men will dream dreams. Even on my servants, both men and women, I will pour out my Spirit in those days, and they will prophesy'"* (Acts 2:17-18).

Prayer: Dad in heaven, thank you that your Word promises that you will pour out your Spirit in me so that I will prophesy, see visions, and dream dreams. Awaken my spirit to receive and understand what you are going to pour out in me. What do you want to show me, Lord? Your daughter is listening and receiving.

Journal:

_____

_____

_____

_____

_____

_____

_____

LET'S CHAT... ABOUT ORGANIZING THE LAUNDRY ROOM

Well, you are off to an amazing start! Let me be the first to congratulate you. You've made it to Day 11, which means you are over the half-way point on your journey to a total home makeover. Keep going, because the journey to home order isn't over yet. Are you ready to have an efficient and organized laundry room? You know, I have to admit that this room is my own personal weakness. I have a tendency to pile things on my dryer. Yuck. Doing laundry is just more pleasant when everything is tidy. So, today's challenge is to get your laundry room in a neat and functional condition. Let's take a look at your laundry room.

Identify activity zones. Here are the common activities that take place in a functional laundry room.

- ☼ Sorting Laundry Zone
- ☼ Washing & Drying Zone
- ☼ Folding & Ironing Zone

Think about Smarter Routines. The first thing you'll want to do is drop your clothes into the hamper (Sorting Laundry Zone). A hamper organizer allows you to sort as you drop. If you have two compartments in your hamper, you can place dirty white clothes into one compartment and your colors into the other compartment. This saves you a step. The hamper should be close to the washer so that you can easily start a load.

Next, you'll reach for your laundry soap (Washing & Drying Zone). Having a shelf or a cupboard directly above your washer and dryer is a great way to hold soaps and softeners. Place the laundry soap near the washer. Near the laundry soap will be the fabric softener, your next step. You'll need to dry your clothes either in the dryer or on a rack or clothes line.

After your clothes are properly dried, you'll need to either fold or hang them on hangers (Folding & Ironing Zone). If you hang up most of your clothes, I recommend having a bar with hangers in your laundry room. You can purchase a roll-away bar for very little at your local department store, or you can attach a bar to the underside of your shelf or cupboard. **Note**: Save yourself a step; don't fold clothes that you plan on hanging up in your closet. Instead, hang them up right away. It will be helpful to have a table, countertop, or some kind of smooth surface for folding clothes. Finally, don't forget to put away your clean clothes. Do you see how you will want to arrange your laundry room according to saving you time and steps? Ironing boards usually don't have to come out all the time, so they can be stored farther away.

Tip! One reader shared that she puts clean clothes in baskets, and each family member is responsible for putting away their own laundry.

What to Keep

- ☼ Washer
- ☼ Dryer
- ☼ Clothes hamper/organizer
- ☼ Closet, cupboard, or shelf to store laundry detergents
- ☼ Iron & ironing board
- ☼ Laundry basket
- ☼ Rack with hangers (optional)

Let's put that professional organizer hat back on and get started organizing the laundry room. **Use the "Design your Space" guide to keep you on track.** You can do it!

GET MOVING!

✓ Complete your morning and evening routines.

✓ Complete your daily Charming Chore.

✓ Remember to initiate your Family's To-Do Time.

✓ Organize laundry room.

From my Life

In the summer of 2001, my husband Nevin and I decided to move back home to Pennsylvania from Virginia. We packed up our things in a pick-up truck. In the process, a bungee cord that Nevin was using to tie down our boxes flew loose and hit me right by my eye. Nevin took me to the emergency room, where I received a few stitches and was sent on my way. Other than a black and blue eye, I looked fine. We finished our move back to Pennsylvania. My parents were kind enough to let us move into their home temporarily until we found a place to stay.

My parents used to go to the laundromat. I could have done the same, except a friend of mine (I'll say Sarah) said we could use her washer and dryer while she was away on vacation. What a lovely offer. I gladly accepted. So, my husband and I packed up our dirty laundry in bags and headed out to Sarah's house.

I knew where everything was in Sarah's home, so it didn't take me long to get the laundry started. I sat down to watch some television while I waited for my clothes to wash. My husband noticed that Sarah's dad was out back, mowing her lawn.

Nevin went outside to say hello. Nevin waved to Sarah's dad, John. John waved back, smiled, and kept mowing. Nevin came back inside and helped me with the laundry.

What we didn't know was that John was not wearing his glasses. He just saw a strange man waving at him and wondered who could be at his daughter's house while she was on vacation. John soon went home to his wife and told her about the strange man. They didn't know what to do. All they knew was that there was a strange man at Sarah's home with a strange car in the driveway that had "Virginia plates." They also noticed that the dryer was going as well.

Can you imagine their thoughts? *A thief is not only stealing from Sarah, but also doing laundry!* A little later as I was folding laundry, the doorbell rang. I opened the door and looked out with my black and blue eye. There stood a police officer! You can imagine my surprise. Luckily, Sarah's mother recognized me and hollered from the driveway, "Never mind, we know them!" That was the most exciting laundry experience I've ever had.

Design your Laundry Room

Step 1: Choose Activity Zones and Layout

_____

_____

_____

_____

Step 2: Clear and Sort into 3 Piles (Trash, Give-away, or Keep)

Give-away Items	Est. Value	Give-away Items	Est. Value

Step 3: Choose Containers

Keep Piles (Like Items)   Est. Size   Container Solution (Budget)

_____

_____

_____

_____

_____

_____

_____

_____

_____

_____

_____

_____

_____

_____

_____

_____

_____

_____

_____

_____

_____

_____

_____

Stain Removal Chart

Blood Stains	Rinse with cold water immediately. If handy, try club soda. For dried stains, blot with hydrogen peroxide.
Coffee/Tea	Apply mild dish soap and rinse with warm water. Blot with vinegar and rinse.
Food Stains	Blot with mild dish soap. Rinse and launder.
Ink Stains	Apply hairspray or rubbing alcohol. Launder as normal.
Pet Urine	Blot with paper towels. Apply vinegar/water solution. Rinse.
Wine Stains	Apply salt. Rinse with water and dry.

Homemade Laundry Detergent

Ingredients:

- ☼ 3.1 oz. bar Ivory soap (Ivory is chosen because it's all natural. You may use a soap of your choice)
- ☼ 1 cup 20 Mule Team Borax
- ☼ ½ cup Arm & Hammer Washing Soda (not to be confused with baking soda)
- ☼ Water

Tools: 5 gallon container, knife, large pot, long stirring stick/spoon

Instructions: Shave the soap into small strips and place in pot with 5 cups of water. Bring the water just shy of a boil and stir until the soap is completely melted. Pour 3 gallons of hot water into the 5-gallon container and add soap mixture. Stir. Add ½ cup of washing soda and stir until dissolved. Add 1 cup of borax and stir again until dissolved. Optional: If you like fragrant detergent, add a few drops of your favorite essential oil. You will have a huge container of hot soapy looking water. Cover the container and let cool overnight. Once cooled, it will gel and will look lumpy and watery. You can put your homemade Detergent into smaller containers for convenience. **Usage**: Stir before use. One-half cup per laundry load. **Yield**: 110 loads

Homemade Fabric Softener: Distilled white vinegar can be used as a fabric softener. After drying in dryer, it leaves no smell or chemical residue in your clothes.

Day 12

DAILY RENEWAL

Bible: *"I (Jesus) have made Your Name known to them and revealed Your character and Your very Self, and I will continue to make [You] known, that the **love** which You have bestowed upon Me may be in them [felt in their hearts] and that I [Myself] may be in them"* (John 17:26, AMP).

Prayer: Dad in heaven, thank you that Jesus made your Name and tangible love known to all of humankind. Please fill my heart up with your tangible love so that I may leak it out and make your love known to those around me. May I always remember that the "greatest of these is love." I invite you to fill me up with your love today. What is in your heart today? Your daughter is listening.

Journal:

_____

_____

_____

_____

_____

_____

LET'S CHAT... ABOUT ORGANIZING THE HOME OFFICE

Today we're going to tackle the home office. Whether it's just a file box and calculator or a room with a desk and computer, everyone needs a home office—and an organized one at that. Having a home office will set you up for financial success as well, because you're going to have great tracking systems. Let's take a look at your home office.

Activity Zones

✸ Mail System Zone (mail in & mail out)

✸ Bill System Zone (most urgent to least urgent file on top of desk plus a "Pay Bill Center" that holds your checks, a pen, and even your budget)

✸ Filing and Budget Zone (cardboard file box or metal/wooden file box to hold filed receipts, a basket to hold "unfiled" receipts, a budget tracker on paper or computer to see where your money is going)

✸ Time Management Zone (day planner and family calendar, pen, highlighters to color code your time)

✸ Communication Zone (phone, e-mail, thank you and birthday card box)

✸ Other Zones (For those of you with home businesses, you may need to identify other systems, such as people, communication, and product management. Make a list of extra systems that you need to have in place.)

Think about Smarter Routines. You've just come home with the mail. Instead of laying it on the counter, you take it into the office and put it into a wall organizer labeled "mail in." It's desk work day, so you sit down at your desk. You begin by sorting your mail. You throw junk mail into the trash can beside your desk.

Bills. You keep the bills and write their due dates on the return envelopes at the stamp spot. You put the bills in order according to due dates (most urgent to least urgent) and place all the bills in your bill organizer on top of your desk for a visible reminder. Since a few bills are due, you go ahead and make out your checks. You reach for a pen, which is in a little pen canister on top of your desk, and the check book is easily accessed in your "Pay Bills" file or drawer. You pop a stamp on them and place them into your "mail out" box.

Budget. Next, you want to track your spending. You have a little basket labeled "receipts" on your desk where you've placed all your receipts for the week. You register your receipts into a computer program such as Quicken or a checkbook register. You place the receipts that are tax deductible into a **Receipts File.** You'll want to balance your check book to make sure you have enough money in your account to cover all bills and planned shopping.

Correspondence. Complete this week's communication needs, such as returning phone calls, letters, and e-mails. Remember to write birthday and thank you cards.

Plan your Week. You may also want to manage your time by planning your week on your calendar and making any necessary hair or doctor appointments. The calendar will be either on your desk or hanging close by. Can you see how you will want to place things in a logical order so you can complete your desk tasks efficiently? Here are the major systems you will want in place.

What to Keep

✿ For Mail System: In and Outbox for mail

✿ For Bill System: "Most Urgent to Least Urgent" visible file for bills, a place for your checks and pen

✿ For Filing and Budget Tracking: a basket to hold "unfiled" receipts, file box for filing receipts, and a place to store your budget (This could be a paper file for your budget or a computer software program.)

✿ For Time Management: day planner, calendar, pen, highlighters

✿ Other items: pens, calculator. If room allows: desk, chair, computer, trash can.

Tip! For Items you don't have, put them on your Christmas wish list. Post this on a bulletin board or the fridge for handy access.

Okay, it's time to create order in the office. **Get started with the "Design your Space" guide**. You can do it! Roll up your sleeves and get moving.

GET MOVING!

✓ Complete your morning and evening routines.

✓ Complete your daily Charming Chore!

✓ Remember to initiate your Family's To-Do Time!

✓ Organize home office!

Design your Home Office

Step 1: Choose Activity Zones and Layout

_____

_____

_____

_____

Step 2: Clear and Sort into 3 Piles (Trash, Give-away, or Keep)

Give-away Items	Est. Value	Give-away Items	Est. Value

Step 3: Choose Containers

Keep Piles (Like Items)   Est. Size   Container Solution (Budget)

_____

_____

_____

_____

_____

_____

_____

_____

_____

_____

_____

_____

_____

_____

_____

_____

_____

_____

_____

_____

_____

_____

DAILY RENEWAL

Bible: *"For I know the plans I have for you,"* declares the LORD, *"plans to prosper you and not to harm you, plans to give you hope and a future"* (Jeremiah 29:11).

Prayer: Dad in Heaven, You are a good God all the time. You have good things for me, and I can trust that your plans for me are to prosper me and to give me a hope and a future. I receive your plans and your blessings for my family and myself. As I organize my "family room" today, send angels and send blessings that this might be a room where family and friends are touched with your kingdom and your goodness for all time. Give me ideas on how our family room can be a place filled with love and fun. Your daughter is listening.

Journal:

_____

_____

_____

_____

_____

_____

LET'S CHAT... ABOUT ORGANIZING THE FAMILY ROOM

This is the room where you hang out with your family and do the things you love to do together. The functions of the family room really stem from what you love doing together as a family. There can be several activity zones in a family room. Here are a few common ones. Add specific family activities to the list.

Identify Activity Zones

- ☼ Music Zone (piano and violin practice, CD collection and listening)

- ☼ Conversation Zone (a furniture grouping for conversation with each other and guests)

- ☼ Reading Zone (bookcase and books)

- ☼ Movie Night Zone (entertainment center, DVD's, storage)

A Few Things to Consider. What activities does your family enjoy, and what activities do you want to encourage your family to enjoy together? Do you really want television and video games to be the only focal point of your family's time, or do you want to encourage board games and reading as well? There are many enjoyments in the world; the family room is a place to expose your children to those enjoyments.

Think about Smarter Routines. I love the family room because it's where I have enjoyed my most precious earthly gift, family. It's where I listen to my girls practice violin and piano, sit for a spontaneous theatrical production presented by my daughters, and clap madly for hilarious dance performances and puppet shows. It's also a place to eat popcorn on family movie night and enjoy a heart-to-heart chat with my hubby. Think about your family's lifestyle and enjoyments. What activity zones make sense for your family room? **What to Keep.** For each activity zone, you will want to keep essential pieces. For example, for reading you'll need seating, a bookcase, books, and a lamp. For the items you don't have, put them on your wish list and purchase them as your budget allows.

✿ Music Zone (instruments, music books, CDs, and stereo)

✿ Conversation Zone (couch, chairs, coffee table, lamps)

✿ Reading Zone (books, bookcases, lamp, seating)

✿ Movie Night Zone (TV, entertainment stand, DVDs, DVD storage)

Get started organizing your family room with the "Design your Space" guide. Create activity zones, clear, sort, and containerize. In the end, your family room will be a space to enjoy all the family activities you have come to love.

GET MOVING!

✓ Complete your morning and evening routines.

✓ Complete your daily Charming Chore!

✓ Remember to initiate your Family's To-Do Time!

✓ Organize family room.

Design your Family Room

Step 1: Choose Activity Zones and Layout

_____

_____

_____

_____

Step 2: Clear and Sort into 3 Piles (Trash, Give-away, or Keep)

Give-away Items	Est. Value	Give-away Items	Est. Value

Step 3: Choose Containers

Keep Piles (Like Items)   Est. Size   Container Solution (Budget)

_____

_____

_____

_____

_____

_____

_____

_____

_____

_____

_____

_____

_____

_____

_____

_____

_____

_____

_____

_____

_____

_____

DAILY RENEWAL

Bible: *"And he said, 'The God of our forefathers has **destined** and appointed you to come progressively to know His will [to perceive, to recognize more strongly and clearly, and to become better and more intimately acquainted with His will], and to see the Righteous One (Jesus Christ, the Messiah), and to hear a voice from His [own] mouth and a message from His [own] lips"* (Acts 22:14, AMP).

Prayer: Dad in heaven, I praise you because you are not a silent Father, but you've destined me to "come progressively into knowing your will" as recorded in Acts 22:14. Open my ears that I might hear. Give me the eyes and ears of Jesus. Allow me to see people as you see them: precious children. As I organize my kitchen today, reveal to me how I can feed others both physically and spiritually. May my kitchen be a place where your love pours forth. I invite you to progressively allow me to know your perfect will and ways. Your daughter is listening.

Journal:

_____

_____

_____

_____

LET'S CHAT... ABOUT ORGANIZING THE KITCHEN

The kitchen is the center of the home. Wouldn't you agree that when the kitchen is in order, everything else feels manageable? We want your pantry, fridge, and cooking utensils in order so you'll enjoy food preparation more and become more efficient. The kitchen is the most important place to eliminate clutter since this is your biggest "work" station. Remember, the kitchen is not the "catch-all." Why do we love to look at homes in magazines? Because they don't have all the extra clutter! They have only what they need to function well! We may not recognize this as the reason those pictures appeal to us, but deep down inside, we all long for a home that has less clutter and more function and beauty. The good news is that today is the day to create a clutter-free kitchen. Let's take a look at your kitchen!

Activity Zones in the Kitchen

Serving Zone: Location – close to table

- Cupboard 1 – top shelf for specialty glasses such as wine, middle shelf for mugs, bottom shelf for water glasses (Notice, least used goes on the top)
- Cupboard 2 – dinner plates, salad/dessert plates, bowls, serving dishes
- Drawer 1 – silverware, serving pieces

Food Prep & Cooking Zone: Location – close to fridge, stove, pantry, and counter

- Cupboard 1 – include cutting board, knives, measuring cups and spoons, mixing bowls, casserole dishes

☼ Cupboard 2 – pots and pans

☼ Cupboard 3 – spices organized in alphabetical order

☼ Countertops – utensil jar to hold wooden spoons, spatulas, whisk, etc.

☼ Drawer 1 – pot holders, cookbooks, meal planner

Baking Zone: Location – close to oven, pantry, and counter

☼ Pantry – flour, sugar, baking powder, and other baking items stored together. **Tip!** Put brown sugar and powdered sugar in plastic storage containers. Group nuts, chocolate chips, and coconut together.

Think about Smarter Routines. In the morning, you'll come to the kitchen, unload the dishwasher, and put the clean dishes away. You'll want the dishwasher to be close to your serving zone (cups, dishes, and silverware). You might set the table next. Is your serving zone close to the table also?

Next, you'll prepare breakfast and thaw a meat for dinner. The food prep zone should be close to your fridge, stove, and food prep cupboards. Next, you might fill your dishwasher again, wipe your counters, and be done.

In the evening, it's time to make dinner. You'll go to your food prep zone. Everything in this zone should be fairly close. You'll want food prep tools, your pantry and fridge items, the countertop, and stove. Clean-up might be as simple as filling the dishwasher and running it. Generally speaking, if you group your zones together, it will feel more efficient in the kitchen. Here are a few more tips to consider!

Tip! Totally clear off your counters. All paper needs to disappear. If you have a habit of laying mail on the counter, get a box or basket and label it "mail." This goes in your office.

Tip! Put only the things you use daily back on your counter (coffee maker, microwave, utensil bin). Let's keep all knickknacks off for now. You want a clean, crisp feel to the area you are using to prepare food. One exception would be a single vase of flowers.

What to Keep. If we were lucky, we would have had a list like this when we registered for our wedding! Many things we purchase for the kitchen just aren't essential. Here's what a well-stocked kitchen should have:

1. Cooking Essentials:

   ✿ Tools: wooden spoons, rubber spatulas, turner, whisk, ice cream scoop, vegetable peeler, tongs, kitchen shears, cheese grater, dry and liquid measuring cups, measuring spoons, mixing bowl set, colander, cooling rack, apple slicer

   ✿ Cookware: large stockpot, three-quart saucepan, two-quart saucepan, skillet

   ✿ Cutlery: chef knife, paring knife, carving knife, serrated knife, cutting board, knife block for storage

   ✿ Baking: roaster, pizza pan and pizza cutter, 12-cup muffin pan, cookie sheet, cookie spatula, two round cake pans, bread pan

   ✿ Small appliances: microwave, food processor, blender, coffee maker/grinder, toaster

   ✿ Large appliances: oven, refrigerator, dishwasher

   ✿ Storage: pantry/closet, cupboards, drawers

2. Serving Essentials

   ✿ Table settings: flatware (setting of eight), flatware serving spoons, dish set (setting of eight that includes bowl, salad/

dessert plate, dinner plate, mug), cloth napkins (setting of eight), tablecloth and/or place mats, carafe/pitcher, water glasses (setting of eight), and an optional set of eight wine goblets

☼ Serving dishes: serving bowls and spoons, appetizer server (chips and dip, etc.), platter, gravy server, cream, sugar, butter server, salt and pepper shakers

3. Furniture Essentials: a seating area (bar and bar stools or table and chairs)

Get started with the "Design your Space" guide. Roll up your sleeves and put that professional hat on. Let's get your kitchen de-cluttered. You can do it.

GET MOVING!

✓ Complete your morning and evening routines.
✓ Complete your daily Charming Chore!
✓ Remember to initiate your Family's To-Do Time!
✓ Add items you need to your wish list!
✓ Organize kitchen!

From my Life

Here is a recent kitchen memory. My daughter, Chloe, at age five had a tendency to get silly during homework. One evening she was sitting at our kitchen bar identifying coins. When she got to the nickel, she said, "Oh, nickel! Like nickel head!" I knew she meant knucklehead, but I didn't say a word.

Design your Kitchen

Step 1: Choose Activity Zones and Layout

_____

_____

_____

_____

Step 2: Clear and Sort into 3 Piles (Trash, Give-away, or Keep)

Give-away Items	Est. Value	Give-away Items	Est. Value

Step 3: Choose Containers

Keep Piles (Like Items)   Est. Size   Container Solution (Budget)

_____

_____

_____

_____

_____

_____

_____

_____

_____

_____

_____

_____

_____

_____

_____

_____

_____

_____

_____

_____

_____

_____

_____

_____

DAILY RENEWAL

Bible: *"We are assured and know that [God being a **partner** in their labor] all things work together and are [fitting into a plan] for good to and for those who love God and are called according to [His] design and purpose"* (Romans 8:28, AMP).

Prayer: Dad in heaven, as I organize the dining room today, I think about communing with family, which includes you. Look into all the corners of my heart and shine light into the dark and hidden places so that I may love you with all of my heart. Help me to love you more and more and keep me from running from anything that is hidden. I know you will forgive every sin and dark place within me. Bring me into a deeper communion with you. May my dining room be a daily ritual of communing with family. Bring intimacy and love into our home and our hearts. As we dine, reveal our design and purpose. Your daughter is listening.

Journal:

_____

_____

_____

_____

_____

LET'S CHAT... ABOUT ORGANIZING THE DINING ROOM

Bon appétit! For guests or for family, the dining room is primarily for ... well, dining. From formal to casual, the dining room is a great place to entertain. You want friends and family to feel like they want to stay for awhile. It's that cozy feeling of good food and great conversation.

Activity Zone

☼ Dining Zone – dining and conversation with family and friends, serving on buffet

Think about Smarter Routines. As you consider how your dining room will be used, think about having easy walking paths for family and friends. Are the extra serving dishes close by and convenient? People will come in, sit down, and relax. Can you easily set the table, serve, and clear? Think about how you want to use this room as you create your layout.

Keep essentials.

☼ Table and chairs

☼ Buffet

☼ Linens

☼ Dishes for entertaining (plates, flatware, glasses, wine glasses, serving utensils, serving plates, and bowls)

☼ Wine rack/server

☼ Party supplies

Get started organizing the dining room with the "Design your Space" guide.

GET MOVING!

✓ Complete your morning and evening routines.

✓ Complete your daily Charming Chore.

✓ Remember to initiate your Family's To-Do Time.

✓ Add items you need to your wish list.

✓ Organize dining room.

✓ Give yourself a reward, check in with partner, and post your greatest success at Http://totalhomemakeover.com .

Design your Dining Room

Step 1: Choose Activity Zones and Layout

_____

_____

_____

_____

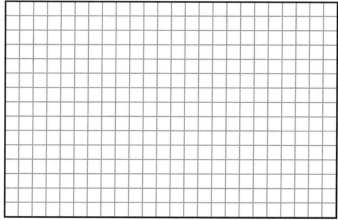

Step 2: Clear and Sort into 3 Piles (Trash, Give-away, or Keep)

Give-away Items	Est. Value	Give-away Items	Est. Value

Step 3: Choose Containers

Keep Piles (Like Items)	Est. Size	Container Solution (Budget)

YOUR THIRD GIFT

"You're organizing
Like the pros,
Assess, toss, sort, and store
Has become your favorite chore,
"Stuff is the enemy" is now your motto,
Take your reward
From my trousseau!"

Treasure Trousseau

1. Shop! Purchase a needed home essential.
2. Glamour! Accessorize your favorite outfit. Use what you have.
3. Pamper! Listen to relaxation music while reading a fun book in bed.
4. Renew! Spend time by the ocean, lake, or river! Journal.
5. Inspire! Watch an inspiring movie such as Facing the Giants.
6. Utopia! Get in the "secret place" with your Heavenly Father.

DAILY RENEWAL

Bible: *Jesus said, "... To you has been entrusted the mystery of the kingdom of God [that is, [b]the secret counsels of God which are hidden from the ungodly]; but for those outside [[c]of our circle] everything becomes a parable"* (Mark 4:11, AMP).

Prayer: Dad in heaven, I am grateful to Jesus for dying on a cross to pay for my return into your amazing kingdom of love and light. I am amazed that you entrust the mysteries of your heavenly kingdom to me. I invite you to reveal your kingdom as I sleep upon my bed at night and as I wake and read your Word. Help me to understand my part in your great harvest. I love you. Your daughter is listening.

Journal:

_____

_____

_____

_____

_____

_____

_____

LET'S CHAT... ABOUT ORGANIZING THE MASTER BEDROOM

Congratulations on completing three weeks of radical change! I'm so excited to tackle your master bedroom. This is the place where you want to unwind and rest. This is your personal sanctuary. If at all possible, you want to eliminate anything that looks like work from this area. If any kind of clutter comes to mind, jot that down as something that needs to be cleared. What are you doing in this space? In the evening, you may wish to be able to read your favorite book in your comfy pajamas while listening to soft music. In the morning, you may want to quickly find a great outfit in your organized closet and be off for the day. Let's take a look at your master bedroom!

Activity Zones

- ☼ **Ready for Bed Zone**. Put dirty clothes in hamper and use the PJ drawer for getting ready for bed.

- ☼ **Resting Zone**. Get into your bed, read a book, set the alarm, turn out the lamp, and go to sleep.

- ☼ **Dressing Zone**. Get up, go to closet, and be able to quickly pull together an outfit, check your look in the mirror, and get out the door. Note: We will organize your master wardrobe tomorrow. But you will still want to identify a location for your Dressing Zone.

Think about Smarter Routines. In the morning, you jump out of bed with a song in your heart and a spring to your steps—or maybe not. Either way, you have to get ready for your day. A smarter routine means you have a dressing zone. All your clothes are easy to access in the same area. In the evening, you need to get ready for bed. Go to your PJ zone and get comfy.

The hamper is close by, and you drop your dirty clothes in it. You then snuggle down into bed and read. Your books are next to the bed for easy access. When designing your layout, think about a logical order to your routine.

Essential Items for each Zone

Get Ready for Bed Zone

☼ Hamper

☼ PJ drawer

Resting Zone

☼ Bed

☼ Two night stands (Idea! Two small bookcases)

☼ Trunk (optional, for extra blanket storage)

☼ Two lamps on night stands

☼ Alarm clock/CD player

☼ CD storage (drawer or photo box)

☼ Phone (optional)

☼ Books

Dressing Zone

☼ Closet

☼ Wardrobe/Dresser

☼ Full-length Mirror

☼ Master Wardrobe (We will organize that tomorrow.)

Get started organizing your master bedroom with the "Design your Space" guide. It might help to draw a sketch of an efficient routine. Know where each zone will be. Then, change things around to flow efficiently. If you need an item such as a hamper, how can you problem solve? Do you already have something in your home that would serve your purpose? Do you need to add anything new to your shopping wish list? Remember, you can get things over time and use temporary solutions. Now, let's organize your master bedroom.

GET MOVING!

- ✓ Complete your morning and evening routines.
- ✓ Complete your daily Charming Chore!
- ✓ Remember to initiate your Family's To-Do Time!
- ✓ Add items you need to your wish list!
- ✓ Organize the master bedroom!

Design your Master Bedroom

Step 1: Choose Activity Zones and Layout

_____

_____

_____

_____

Step 2: Clear and Sort into 3 Piles (Trash, Give-away, or Keep)

Give-away Items   Est.Value   Give-away Items   Est.Value

Step 3: Choose Containers

Keep Piles (Like Items)   Est. Size   Container Solution (Budget)

DAILY RENEWAL

Bible: "*So we are Christ's **ambassadors**, God making His appeal as it were through us. We [as Christ's personal representatives] beg you for His sake to lay hold of the divine favor [now offered you] and be reconciled to God*" (2 Corinthians 5:20, AMP).

Prayer: Dad in heaven, I recognize that I am an ambassador or spokesperson for your kingdom in this foreign country called "earth." Give me wisdom with my words so that they always represent what you are saying. As I organize my wardrobe and as I dress each day, may this be a reminder to me of my role as an ambassador for the King of kings, Jesus. May I communicate the divine favor (through Jesus' death and resurrection) that is offered to others so that all may be reconciled to God. May I always remain humble and confess every sin so that my heart remains reconciled to you. Help me to live out my ambassadorship for Christ well. Reveal your plans for me. Your daughter is listening.

Journal:

_____

_____

_____

_____

LET'S CHAT... ABOUT THE MASTER WARDROBE

Clothing—one of my favorite subjects! If you're like the old me, you go shopping for clothes and buy what appeals to you. I used to do that. I'd end up with too many shirts and too few pants! Does this sound familiar? A well planned wardrobe only requires a few key pieces and doesn't take tons of money or require much storage space.

Today, I want to chat with you about the "Master Wardrobe." You can check off what you already have and begin a Master Shopping List (Page 101) of the things you really need. Keep a copy of this in your purse. Then, the next time you go shopping, you'll stay focused on your true needs!

Master Wardrobe. The building blocks of your wardrobe are your pants, accent jackets, and skirts. Just like a couch, you want these basics to be in neutral colors. Then, you can introduce fun, trendy colors in your shirts and accessories. Let's begin by choosing your basic summer and winter colors. Choose neutrals. For summer, you might choose tan, white, cream, or black. For winter, you might choose black, navy, or chocolate. You will build your wardrobe around these colors. They should flatter your skin tone. I personally love black as my neutral because it matches almost everything in every season and is slimming.

My Basic Summer Color: _____

My Basic Winter Color: _____

The Basic Jacket. You don't have to be on a business trip to wear a jacket. It's my favorite article of clothing! It can be worn over shirts. I like my accent jackets with some built in curve and feminine details. Choose one that suits your personality.

- ☼ Summer jacket (in lighter neutral color and a summer fabric like linen)
- ☼ Winter jacket (darker neutral and heavier fabric)
- ☼ Denim jacket (optional – choose one you absolutely love. Great for a weekend look!)

The Basic Sweater. (Choose a flattering shape that fits well. Look for fun details.)

- ☼ Summer sweater (light neutral such as cream, light fabric in short or mid-length sleeve)
- ☼ Winter sweater (darker neutral in warm fabric)

Renee's Shopping Tip! If you don't absolutely love it on your body right now, don't buy it. For purchases over $100, sleep on it. Twelve hours will give you perspective on your true needs.

The Shirts. Your shirts can be worn alone or layered under your accent jackets or sweaters. Shirts that are longer, hitting around the thigh, are often more flattering for most body shapes!

- ☼ Ruffle shirt (with feminine detail around neckline – choose a color that looks great under jacket)
- ☼ Lace shirt (again with feminine detail – introduce a fun color)
- ☼ Silk shirt in complementary color
- ☼ White tank (long enough to hit around the hips for a slim look – use this to layer under other shirts)

☼ 5 tees or tanks (Choose your favorite skin-flattering colors. Get some variety and even fun trendy details. You will want to change these out yearly. Again, make sure they are long enough!)

☼ Older tees (for exercising)

The Pants. Curvy fit with no pleats is almost always more flattering and slimming! Also, make sure they are long enough to add length to your legs!

☼ 2 basic summer pants (tan, beige, or even black)

☼ 2 basic winter pants (black, gray, chocolate, or navy)

☼ 2 jeans (Snug-fitting pants show off fat. Rather, choose a size that fits just right.)

☼ 1 Pair of exercise pants used only for just that! **Tip!** No sweats unless you're sweating.

The Shorts

☼ 2 pairs capri pants or longer shorts in neutral colors such as black or beige

The Skirts

☼ 1 summer skirt (lighter fabric in summer neutral – choose flattering length)

☼ 1 winter skirt (heavier fabric in winter neutral)

The Dress

☼ 1 summer dress with color and character in a flattering shape that could be paired with your summer accent jacket

☼ 1 winter dress with color and flair in a flattering shape that could be paired with your winter accent jacket

☼ 1 little black dress (for black tie events)

The Shoes

☼ 1 dressy summer shoe in your summer basic color

☼ 1 semi-casual summer shoe in a summer basic color

☼ 1 dressy winter shoe in your winter basic color

☼ 1 semi-casual winter shoe in a winter basic color

☼ 1 pair of dress boots (in winter basic color – looks great with winter skirt, dress, and capri pants)

☼ 1 pair of comfortable walking shoes (sneakers)

The Purse

☼ 1 summer bag (in your basic summer color)

☼ 1 winter bag (in your basic winter color)

☼ 1 trendy fun bag (in accent color you love – try gold or silver)

☼ 1 little clutch (in black, gold, or silver to match little black dress)

The Scarf

☼ 1 summer scarf (accent your shirts – think texture and design)

☼ 1 winter scarf

☼ 1 winter scarf to accent winter coat

The Belt
☼ 1 fun accent belt in silver or gold

The Costume Jewelry
☼ 1 long necklace in silver or gold with matching earrings

☼ 1 necklace in summer basic colors with matching earrings

☼ 1 necklace in winter basic colors with matching earrings

☼ 1 fun ring

The Fine Jewelry
☼ 1 necklace in silver or gold with matching earrings (complement little black dress)

☼ 1 strand of pearls with matching earrings

☼ 1 silver or gold ring

The Coats
☼ 1 summer coat (choose basic summer color or fun color – for rain or cooler weather)

☼ 1 winter coat (How about a wool pea coat in a basic winter color such as charcoal gray? You can dress this up or down!)

After looking at the master wardrobe list, you're probably thinking, "*No wonder I never have anything to wear!*" Obviously, you'll need to adjust your wardrobe to your lifestyle. But these bare bones basics are a must!

Identify your Key Pieces to Keep. Start at the top of the master wardrobe list. If you already have a great summer jacket in a summer neutral, it's flattering, and you love it, put that on your "keep" pile and check it off the list. Then go on to the winter jacket and do the same. If you have a lot of extra jackets, sort them as you go. Trash, give-away, or keep. However, you can't keep fifty jackets you absolutely love if you have a small closet. Decide on your top five jackets if room allows. Once you've gone through all your jackets, move on to choosing your key summer and winter sweaters. Obviously, if you haven't worn any article in the past year, it's out of here! Keep going until you've completed the list.

Identify your Dressing Zone. Let me help you with this. If possible, choose your closet and make this your dressing zone so you're not wasting steps bouncing from closet to dresser to wardrobe. The dresser could hold off-season clothes and extras. Within the closet, there will be zones. A shirt zone, a pant zone, etc. It's easiest to pair like items together and then place them in order of the rainbow. Your shirts, from left to right, might be arranged in groups of red and pink, orange, yellow, green, blue, purple, black, and white.

Think about Smarter Routines. I've arranged this closet according to how we often dress ourselves. Is it a pant or skirt day? Now, select a flattering top. Add a jacket or sweater. Add accessories such as shoes, jewelry, and hand bag.

Create Zones. Now, you'll want to go through and add your zones to the closet. I highly recommend adding a hanging bar extension found at any department store. How about some simple shelves or even plastic drawers to organize your accessories? Put your wardrobe back. If you still have too many clothes and your closets are bursting, you'll want to edit out a few more articles. Try to fill no more then eighty percent. What don't you love? What do you have in excess?

I believe you have a handle on how to create a master wardrobe. I'll leave you with these parting words today. It's time to roll up your sleeves and get moving. You can do it!

GET MOVING!

✓ Complete your morning and evening routines.

✓ Complete your daily Charming Chore!

✓ Remember to initiate your Family's To-Do Time!

✓ Add items you need to your wish list!

✓ Organize your master wardrobe!

Design your Wardrobe

Step 1: Choose Activity Zones and Layout

_____

_____

_____

_____

Step 2: Clear and Sort into 3 Piles (Trash, Give-away, or Keep)

Give-away Items	Est. Value	Give-away Items	Est. Value

Step 3: Choose Containers

Keep Piles (Like Items)   Est. Size   Container Solution (Budget)

_____

_____

_____

_____

_____

_____

_____

_____

_____

_____

_____

_____

_____

_____

_____

_____

_____

_____

_____

_____

_____

_____

My Master Wardrobe Shopping List
(Place copy in purse)

_____

_____

_____

_____

_____

_____

_____

_____

_____

_____

_____

_____

_____

_____

_____

_____

_____

_____

_____

_____

_____

_____

DAILY RENEWAL

Bible: *Jesus said, "For wherever two or three are **gathered** (drawn together as My followers) in (into) My **name**, there I AM in the midst of them"* (Matthew 18:20, AMP)

Prayer: Dad in heaven, as I organize my children's bedroom today, I claim your promises. Whenever I gather with my children each evening, you are in our midst. Bless our time of Bible reading and prayer each evening. Awaken our spirits to your Holy Spirit. We invite your Holy Spirit to be in our midst, to be our teacher and guide. We love you. Let it be so (Amen).

Journal:

_____

_____

_____

_____

_____

_____

_____

_____

_____

LET'S CHAT... ABOUT ORGANIZING THE CHILDREN'S BEDROOM

From changing into PJ's, reading and resting, and dressing for school, the children's bedroom needs to feel like a peaceful sanctuary. If possible, keep toys in another room. Getting your child's room in order really is pretty simple. Let's take a look at the Zones.

Identify the Zones

☼ PJ Zone

☼ Resting Zone

☼ Dressing Zone

Think about Smarter Routines

At bedtime, your child will go to the PJ zone and change into PJ's. Then, it's off to the resting zone where you might read together, set the alarm clock, turn off the lamp, and say goodnight. In the morning, your child can get up and go to dressing zone. Try to keep the dressing zone in one location. You can organize a child's wardrobe similar to your own master wardrobe.

Tip! I have my children pick out their outfits the night before school and hang them on hooks on the wall. This helps their morning routine move along more quickly.

Keep essentials

☼ PJ Zone - PJ drawer, hamper

☼ Resting Zone - bed, bedding, husband/pillows, lamps, night stands, books, alarm clock, CD player, and CDs

☼ Dressing Zone - organized closet, full-length mirror, dressers

Notice that like items are paired together. Plus, the items are arranged from left to right by colors of the rainbow (red/pink, orange, yellow, green, blue, purple, and then brown, black, and white).

Children's Wardrobe Essentials

FOR HER

Tops

- ☼ Jacket - jean or neutral
- ☼ Summer sweater in neutral such as cream
- ☼ Winter sweater in darker neutral
- ☼ Colorful shirts (5-10 per season)

Bottoms

- ☼ 1 neutral slack
- ☼ 3-5 jeans
- ☼ 3-5 winter leggings in fun colors (coordinate with shirts)
- ☼ 3-5 summer shorts in fun colors (coordinate with shirts)
- ☼ 2 skirts (jean and neutral)

Dresses

- ☼ 1 formal occasion dress for holidays, birthday parties, etc.
- ☼ 3-5 casual, seasonal, colorful dresses

Shoes

- ☼ 2 seasonal shoes in neutral (one dress and one casual)
- ☼ Sneakers

Accessories

- ☼ 5-10 pair of socks (a few should have frills)
- ☼ 2 pair stockings
- ☼ Fun scarf, purse, jewelry, and hair barrettes in an accent color such as gold or silver

☼ Lip gloss and perfume

Outer Wear & Under Wear

☼ Spring/fall jacket (get more mileage when it doubles as a rain coat)

☼ Winter coat (Choose a sharp one that can be worn to school and for winter play. You may be able to get one size bigger and get two years' worth of wear out of it.)

☼ Matching scarf, hat, and gloves

☼ 10+ pairs of underwear

FOR HIM

Tops

☼ 1 dress jacket in a dark neutral (chocolate corduroy)

☼ 2 sweater vests in neutrals (navy and tan)

☼ 5-10 colorful shirts

bottoms

☼ 2 neutral slacks

☼ 3-5 jeans

☼ 3-5 summer shorts (jean and tan)

Shoes

☼ 2 seasonal shoes in neutral (one dress and one casual)

☼ Sneakers

Outer Wear & Under Wear

☼ Spring/fall jacket (get more mileage when it doubles as a rain coat)

☼ Winter coat (Choose a sharp one that can be worn to school and for winter play. You may be able to get one size bigger and get two years' worth of wear out of it.)

☼ Matching scarf, hat, and gloves

☼ 10+ pairs of underwear

Get started with the "Design your Space" guide. You will need to make decisions on a smart layout for your child's room. Where will the PJ zone be? Where will the resting zone be? How can the books, lamp, and alarm clock be close to the bed? For the dressing zone, consider organizing the closet as I've suggested.

As you're creating zones, you'll also be de-cluttering. When you touch something, quickly assess if it needs to stay here or move on. Remember to create three piles as you clear and sort: Keep, toss, or donate. It will save you time if you sort "keep" items into like piles such as socks with socks. You may not have all the essential items you need right now. That's okay. Make a wish list for future purchases as your budget allows. For now, creatively problem solve. Can a large square basket turned on its side serve as a nightstand and book holder? You can have order on a small budget.

GET MOVING!

✓ Complete your morning and evening routines.

✓ Complete your daily Charming Chore.

✓ Remember to initiate your Family's To-Do Time.

✓ Add items you need to your wish list.

✓ Organize child's bedroom.

Design your Child's Bedroom

Step 1: Choose Activity Zones and Layout

_____

_____

_____

_____

Step 2: Clear and Sort into 3 Piles (Trash, Give-away, or Keep)

Give-away Items	Est. Value	Give-away Items	Est. Value
_____	_____	_____	_____
_____	_____	_____	_____
_____	_____	_____	_____
_____	_____	_____	_____
_____	_____	_____	_____
_____	_____	_____	_____
_____	_____	_____	_____

Step 3: Choose Containers

Keep Piles (Like Items)   Est. Size   Container Solution (Budget)

_____

_____

_____

_____

_____

_____

_____

_____

_____

_____

_____

_____

_____

_____

_____

_____

_____

_____

_____

_____

_____

_____

DAILY RENEWAL

Bible: *"The Lord told him, I have heard your **prayer** and supplication which you have made before Me; I have hallowed this house which you have built, and I have put My Name [and My Presence] there forever. My eyes and My heart shall be there perpetually"* (1 Kings 9:3, AMP)

Prayer: Dad in heaven, I am your child, and you hear my prayers and supplications. Today, I pour out my heart before you. This is what is on my heart… Thank you for hearing me. Please give me a special gift that I might know that I am seen and heard. Let it be so (Amen).

Journal:

_____

_____

_____

_____

_____

_____

_____

_____

LET'S CHAT... ABOUT ORGANIZING THE BATHROOM

Good morning! You have made tremendous progress! The next thing we want to think about is the bathroom. Now this is where you probably head first thing in the morning to grab a shower and primp for the day. Do you have this arranged in a logical order? Are things easy to find, or do you waste time hunting down your hairspray and tooth paste? Let's take a look at your bathroom.

Identify Zones

* Shower Zone
* Primp Zone (Hair, Makeup, Nails)
* Potty Zone

Think about Smarter Routines

Shower Zone: Grab your towel, put dirty clothes in hamper, and shower. You'll wash hair with shampoo and conditioner, wash body with soap, and possibly shave. Ah! Fresh and clean!

Primp Zone: Apply lotion, perfume, and makeup. Then, dry and style your hair. Extra time? Touch up your nails.

Potty Zone: A necessary stop in our day. Don't forget to have toilet paper, wipes for kids, menstrual supplies, and reading material handy.

What to Keep
Shower Zone:

* Towels
* Wash cloths
* Hamper
* Shampoo

☼ Conditioner

☼ Soap and body wash

☼ Back scrubber

☼ Razor & men's face mirror for shaving

Primp Zone

☼ Body lotions and perfumes

☼ Makeup

☼ Hair styling tools and products

☼ Nail supplies

Potty Zone

☼ Toilet paper

☼ Wet wipes for kids

☼ Menstrual supplies

☼ Reading material in reading basket

Get started with the "Design your Space" guide.
As you pull things out, assess, sort into Keep piles or Donate/
Toss. *Oh, here is my old crimper from 7th grade.* Toss! *Here are twenty-
five lipsticks.* Keep only five to ten. Try to put all needed essentials
close to each zone. For example, towels should be in easy reach
from the shower. Do you need a little shower caddy or organizer
to hold shower supplies? It makes sense to place the primp zone
close to the mirror. When you've finished clearing and sorting,
look at your "keep" piles. Do you have proper storage? What
solutions can you come up with? It's time to roll up your sleeves
and get started organizing the bathroom. You can do it.

GET MOVING!

✓ Complete your morning and evening routines.

✓ Complete your daily Charming Chore.

✓ Remember to initiate your Family's To-Do Time.

✓ Add items you need to your wish list.

✓ Organize the bathroom(s).

Design your Bathroom

Step 1: Choose Activity Zones and Layout

_____

_____

_____

_____

Step 2: Clear and Sort into 3 Piles (Trash, Give-away, or Keep)

Give-away Items	Est. Value	Give-away Items	Est. Value

Step 3: Choose Containers

Keep Piles (Like Items)	Est. Size	Container Solution (Budget)

DAILY RENEWAL

Bible: *"The Lord opens the eyes of the blind, the Lord lifts up those who are bowed down, the Lord loves the [uncompromisingly] righteous (those upright in heart and in right standing with Him)"* (Psalm 146:8, AMP).

Prayer: Dear Dad in heaven, Thank you that you open up my eyes. Thank you that you lift me up. Thank you that you have made me righteous (in right standing with you) and that you love me. As I continue to maintain my home and my heart, journey with me and never leave me, as you have promised. May I continue to grow in intimacy with you. Your daughter is listening.

Journal:

_____

_____

_____

_____

_____

_____

LET'S CHAT... ABOUT ORGANIZING THE STORAGE AREA

This is our final day together. It's our grand finale to that functional and easy-to-maintain home. Afterwards, you can follow the maintenance plan at the back of the book or access the maintenance plan at totalhomemakeover.com. The system of order I've presented in this book is less about doing the "perfect thing" every day. It's more of a home management system that allows you to focus on enjoying your relationships, your life, and your true destiny.

Today, we'll focus on organizing our storage areas. There are many supplies we don't use daily. Things like Christmas decorations, lawn and gardening tools, and sports equipment all end up in storage. When we need to find these supplies, it's helpful to actually know where they are. It helps to have storage that is labeled and accessible. That's what we're going to accomplish today. Let's take a look at our Storage Zones! Check off the zones that apply to you.

Identify Storage Zones

☼ Seasonal Decorations Zone

☼ Extra Toys Zone (You can store extra toys in bins and rotate monthly.)

☼ Home Hardware Zone (anything you use to fix up your home, such as extra paint, painting supplies, tools, nails for hanging pictures)

☼ Hobby Zone (What is your hobby? Arts/crafts, sewing, etc.)

☼ Rarely Used Items Zone (The ice cream maker, winter coats, and tennis rackets can go here.)

☼ Lawn and Garden Zone (anything you use to maintain your lawn and gardens)

❂ Automobile Zone (tools used to change your oil and maintain your automobiles)

In general, home storage items can go in the attic, basement, garage, or tool shed. Use plastic tubs in the basement in case of flooding. Lawn, garden, and automobile items would be best stored in the garage or shed.

Clear and Sort

Put all seasonal decorations together in a pile, all extra toys in another pile, etc. Remember to toss and donate as you sort through your items. Have your toss and give-away garbage bags close at hand.

Containerize

Look at the size of your piles and make a list of needed storage totes. If you don't have enough, you could use boxes for now. Add your needs to your shopping wish list. Then, label your boxes on the outside, such as "Christmas Decorations" or "Kitchen Tools."

Get started organizing with "Design your Space" guide.

This has been an amazing journey. As I've walked through this process of organizing my home, I've created a home that is more functional, livable, peaceful, and manageable. I know you will say the same. We should recognize that our lives are always changing and that we will always be in the process. Different zones will be needed throughout our lives.

I hope that you've conceptualized the keys to home order: daily and weekly routine, involving your family with home management, and enjoying organized and functional rooms. Organization is about identifying the activities in our lives and having zones to accomplish those activities. Mostly, I hope you know how great you really are and that the value of an orderly home will free your time and mind to focus more on knowing our God, ourselves, our loved ones, and our gifts.

With a sentimental tear at my eye, I'll remind you one last time to roll up your sleeves and get moving. You can do it!

GET MOVING!

✓ Complete your morning and evening routines.

✓ Complete your daily Charming Chore.

✓ Remember to initiate your Family's To-Do Time.

✓ Add items you need to your wish list.

✓ Organize your storage.

✓ Take your Reward: Celebrate your success with your family and/or your partner.

✓ Go to Http://totalhomemakeover.com and report your success. We would love to hear about your experience. Please tell one way this journey has changed your life for the better.

Design your Storage

Step 1: Choose Activity Zones and Layout

_____

_____

_____

_____

Step 2: Clear and Sort into 3 Piles (Trash, Give-away, or Keep)

Give-away Items	Est. Value	Give-away Items	Est. Value

Step 3: Choose Containers

Keep Piles (Like Items)   Est. Size   Container Solution (Budget)

_____

_____

_____

_____

_____

_____

_____

_____

_____

_____

_____

_____

_____

_____

_____

_____

_____

_____

_____

_____

_____

_____

YOUR FOURTH GIFT

A home with routines,
A family chore chart,
Consistency is all where it starts,
Your rooms now have zones
And with 50% less stuff,
Focus more on your life
And not all the fluff.

Treasure Trousseau

Celebrate and enjoy your organized home.

Spiritual Fun: Anoint and bless your home. Give your home to God and invite His blessing upon it. Ask for His protection and presence in your home.

Record your Success: Involve your children and create a one to two-minute "home video" that shows off your newly transformed home. Make it funny, positive, and entertaining. Post it on YouTube and send the link to nrmetzler@windstream.net. Your success story may be selected for our website to inspire and encourage other women, or you can just e-mail us at nrmetzler@windstream.net and tell us why you loved your total home makeover.

Stay In: Enjoy an "old-fashioned movie" night in your new "clutter-free" home. Order in pizza and take a well-deserved break. Every so often, look around at your home and mentally pat yourself on the back. Before you head for bed, say, "I rock!" at least three times.

Go Out: Celebrate your success by going out and skipping your evening routine. Let someone else wash dishes for the night.

When you arrive back home, everyone in the family can give a big "round of applause" for a job well done.

Home Maintenance Plan

Daily
- ✓ Complete your morning and evening routines.
- ✓ Complete your daily Charming Chore!
- ✓ Remember to initiate your Family's To-Do Time!

Weekly
- ✓ Reward yourself and your family!
- ✓ Remember to plan your week (Sunday nights).

Monthly Re-organize and detail clean one room per month. Re-organize simply means to bring back to the original state of order. Remember your activity zones, avoid backtracking, and store like things together. Detail clean. Start at the top (ceiling lights and cobwebs in the corners), go to the middle (windows, dirt on walls, doors, and door knobs), and finish at the bottom (which is furniture/appliances and floors).

January
- ✓ Re-organize office
- ✓ Detail clean office
- ✓ Start preparing for taxes

February
- ✓ Re-organize laundry room
- ✓ Detail clean laundry room

March
- ✓ Re-organize kitchen

✓ Detail clean kitchen

✓ Remember to clean drawers and cupboards

April

✓ Re-organize porch and foyer

✓ Detail clean porch and foyer

✓ Bring out spring/summer jackets

May

✓ Re-organize dining room

✓ Detail clean dining room

June

✓ Re-organize family room

✓ Detail clean family room

July

✓ Re-organize master bedroom & wardrobe

✓ Detail clean master bedroom

August

✓ Re-organize children's bedroom & wardrobe

✓ Detail clean children's bedroom

September

✓ Re-organize bathroom(s)

✓ Detail clean bathroom(s)

October

✓ Re-organize storage

✓ Detail clean storage

November - Prepare for holidays

December - Enjoy the holidays

MASTER SHOPPING LIST

_____

_____

_____

_____

_____

_____

_____

_____

_____

_____

_____

_____

_____

_____

_____

_____

_____

_____

_____

_____

_____

_____

_____

_____

ONE MONTH
Bonus Planner

Define my Values, Mission Statement, and Goals

1. Complete the Values and Mission Statement Worksheet. Consult your Heavenly Father. I like to ask, "What are you doing, and how can I enter into your plan?" As you consider goals, also look inside your heart. This is more about the desires of your heart and less about why you need to perform.

2. Create goals with a deadline. Give yourself grace.

3. Always remember who is in the driver's seat of life. Hold your plans loosely.

Plan my Month

1. Add the following items and events to the monthly calendar:

a. Schedule and record appointments for this month (hair, doctor, dentist).

b. Schedule events for the month:

__ God events

__ Family events (romantic date w/spouse, school/extra curricular events, family fun)

__ Extended family, friendship, and community events

___ Self events (celebration night or a mom's day out reward, etc.)

2. Create or review your values and mission statement.

3. Create or review your monthly goals. Consult your Creator. Ask, "What are You doing, and how would You like me to enter into your bigger plan?"

4. Schedule in monthly goals with a deadline. Give yourself grace. You should feel a sense of peace about your goals. Example: Finish writing four chapters by end of month.

5. Schedule in a monthly reward for completion of goals (smell the roses).

Plan my Week (Here is a logical order.)

1. Add appointments and events to your weekly calendar.

1. Plan daily renewal time. (6 am - read, pray, praise, journal)

2. Plan morning routine (7 am)

3. Plan daily exercise time (8 am)

4. Plan daily Charming Chore (9 am)

Monday - Meal Plan

Tuesday - Desk Work

Wednesday - Errands

Thursday - Laundry

Friday - Wave Clean

Saturday - Family Day

Sunday - Rest, renew, and seek God (Plan your next week in the evening.)

5. Plan daily goal time (ex. 11 am - write 3 pages today, 1 chapter this wk.)

6. Plan family time (5 – 6 pm, dinner hour, playing in the evening, homework)

7. Plan evening routine (8 pm)

8. Self time (9 pm, read, write, relax)

Plan my Day

1. Your weekly plan will actually guide your daily plan.

2. Review your day for appointments or events.

3. Make a daily to-do list the night before. These are most urgent to least urgent items. This will be things outside your normal routines. (1. Call child's doctor for an appointment. 2. Make special meal for guests coming tonight. 3. Return Aunt Verma's phone call.)

4. Extra time? Spend time just sitting in the presence of the Father. Hearing a friend's heart over the phone. Taking your daughter out for a special lunch...just because. Writing a love note to your spouse. Working a little more on a goal.

Values and Goals Worksheet

My Values! (Write down ten things you value the most in life. Example: relationships, virtues, education in an area, spiritual, physical, career)

_____

_____

_____

_____

_____

_____

_____

My Mission Statement! (Using the list of values above, create a personal mission statement of what you want to accomplish or focus on according to your values. Try to focus on three broader categories. Example: build my relationship with God and family, personally grow, and use my gift of writing.)

_____

_____

_____

_____

_____

_____

_____

My Goals! (Make specific goals that are measurable and have a deadline. Example: I will finish writing my book by April.)

My Spiritual Goals:

_____

_____

_____

_____

My Relationship Goals (family & friends):

_____

_____

_____

_____

My Career/Personal/Educational Goals:

_____

_____

_____

_____

My Health Goals:

_____

_____

_____

_____

My Financial Goals (Tithe 10% and Save 5% of every paycheck):

_____

_____

_____

_____

Monthly Calendar

Month of: _____ Year: _____

M	T	W	T	F	S	S

My Weekly Plan

Week of: _____

Time	Monday	Tuesday	Wednesday	Thursday	Friday
5:00 AM					
6:00 AM					
7:00 AM					
8:00 AM					
9:00 AM					
10:00 AM					
11:00 AM					
NOON					
1:00 PM					
2:00 PM					
3:00 PM					
4:00 PM					
5:00 PM					
6:00 PM					
7:00 PM					
8:00 PM					
9:00 PM					
10:00 PM					

Saturday: _____

Sunday: _____

Color Code: God, Family, Household, Career, Personal, Relationships

Daily To-Do List

	Mon	Tues	Wed	Thurs	Fri
1.	_____	_____	_____	_____	_____
2.	_____	_____	_____	_____	_____
3.	_____	_____	_____	_____	_____
4.	_____	_____	_____	_____	_____
5.	_____	_____	_____	_____	_____
6.	_____	_____	_____	_____	_____

My Weekly Meal Plan

Delicious, Nutritious, and No Time at All!

Week of: _____   Notes (recipe page #s)

Monday

Breakfast: _____

Lunch: _____

Dinner: _____

Tuesday

Breakfast: _____

Lunch: _____

Dinner: _____

Wednesday

Breakfast: _____

Lunch: _____

Dinner: _____

Thursday

Breakfast: _____

Lunch: _____

Dinner: _____

Friday

Breakfast: _____

Lunch: _____

Dinner: _____

Saturday: _____

Sunday: _____

Grocery List

Produce	Canned/ Packaged	Dairy
_____	_____	_____
_____	_____	_____
_____	_____	_____
_____	_____	_____
_____	_____	_____
_____	_____	_____
_____	_____	_____
_____	_____	_____
_____	_____	_____
_____	_____	_____
_____	_____	_____
_____	_____	_____
_____	_____	_____
_____	_____	_____
_____	_____	_____
_____	_____	_____
_____	_____	_____
_____	_____	_____
_____	_____	_____
_____	_____	_____

Grocery List

Meats	Freezer	Other

My Weekly Plan

Week of: _____

Time	Monday	Tuesday	Wednesday	Thursday	Friday
5:00 AM					
6:00 AM					
7:00 AM					
8:00 AM					
9:00 AM					
10:00 AM					
11:00 AM					
NOON					
1:00 PM					
2:00 PM					
3:00 PM					
4:00 PM					
5:00 PM					
6:00 PM					
7:00 PM					
8:00 PM					
9:00 PM					
10:00 PM					

Saturday: _____

Sunday: _____

Color Code: God, Family, Household, Career, Personal, Relationships

Daily To-Do List

	Mon	Tues	Wed	Thurs	Fri
1.					
2.					
3.					
4.					
5.					
6.					

My Weekly Meal Plan

Delicious, Nutritious, and No Time at All!

Week of: _____   **Notes (recipe page #s)**

Monday

Breakfast: _____

Lunch: _____

Dinner: _____

Tuesday

Breakfast: _____

Lunch: _____

Dinner: _____

Wednesday

Breakfast: _____

Lunch: _____

Dinner: _____

Thursday

Breakfast: _____

Lunch: _____

Dinner: _____

Friday

Breakfast: _____

Lunch: _____

Dinner: _____

Saturday: _____

Sunday: _____

Grocery List

Produce	Canned/ Packaged	Dairy
_____	_____	_____
_____	_____	_____
_____	_____	_____
_____	_____	_____
_____	_____	_____
_____	_____	_____
_____	_____	_____
_____	_____	_____
_____	_____	_____
_____	_____	_____
_____	_____	_____
_____	_____	_____
_____	_____	_____
_____	_____	_____
_____	_____	_____
_____	_____	_____
_____	_____	_____
_____	_____	_____

Grocery List

Meats	Freezer	Other
_____	_____	_____
_____	_____	_____
_____	_____	_____
_____	_____	_____
_____	_____	_____
_____	_____	_____
_____	_____	_____
_____	_____	_____
_____	_____	_____
_____	_____	_____
_____	_____	_____
_____	_____	_____
_____	_____	_____
_____	_____	_____
_____	_____	_____
_____	_____	_____
_____	_____	_____
_____	_____	_____
_____	_____	_____

My Weekly Plan

Week of: _____

Time	Monday	Tuesday	Wednesday	Thursday	Friday
5:00 AM					
6:00 AM					
7:00 AM					
8:00 AM					
9:00 AM					
10:00 AM					
11:00 AM					
NOON					
1:00 PM					
2:00 PM					
3:00 PM					
4:00 PM					
5:00 PM					
6:00 PM					
7:00 PM					
8:00 PM					
9:00 PM					
10:00 PM					

Saturday: _____

Sunday: _____

Color Code: God, Family, Household, Career, Personal, Relationships

Daily To-Do List

	Mon	Tues	Wed	Thurs	Fri
1.	_____	_____	_____	_____	_____
2.	_____	_____	_____	_____	_____
3.	_____	_____	_____	_____	_____
4.	_____	_____	_____	_____	_____
5.	_____	_____	_____	_____	_____
6.	_____	_____	_____	_____	_____

My Weekly Meal Plan
Delicious, Nutritious, and No Time at All!

Week of: _____   **Notes (recipe page #s)**

Monday
Breakfast: _____
Lunch: _____
Dinner: _____

Tuesday
Breakfast: _____
Lunch: _____
Dinner: _____

Wednesday
Breakfast: _____
Lunch: _____
Dinner: _____

Thursday
Breakfast: _____
Lunch: _____
Dinner: _____

Friday
Breakfast: _____
Lunch: _____
Dinner: _____

Saturday: _____

Sunday: _____

Grocery List

Produce	Canned/ Packaged	Dairy
_____	_____	_____
_____	_____	_____
_____	_____	_____
_____	_____	_____
_____	_____	_____
_____	_____	_____
_____	_____	_____
_____	_____	_____
_____	_____	_____
_____	_____	_____
_____	_____	_____
_____	_____	_____
_____	_____	_____
_____	_____	_____
_____	_____	_____
_____	_____	_____
_____	_____	_____
_____	_____	_____
_____	_____	_____
_____	_____	_____

Grocery List

Meats	Freezer	Other
_____	_____	_____
_____	_____	_____
_____	_____	_____
_____	_____	_____
_____	_____	_____
_____	_____	_____
_____	_____	_____
_____	_____	_____
_____	_____	_____
_____	_____	_____
_____	_____	_____
_____	_____	_____
_____	_____	_____
_____	_____	_____
_____	_____	_____
_____	_____	_____
_____	_____	_____
_____	_____	_____
_____	_____	_____
_____	_____	_____
_____	_____	_____

My Weekly Plan

Week of: _____

Time	Monday	Tuesday	Wednesday	Thursday	Friday
5:00 AM					
6:00 AM					
7:00 AM					
8:00 AM					
9:00 AM					
10:00 AM					
11:00 AM					
NOON					
1:00 PM					
2:00 PM					
3:00 PM					
4:00 PM					
5:00 PM					
6:00 PM					
7:00 PM					
8:00 PM					
9:00 PM					
10:00 PM					

Saturday: _____

Sunday: _____

Color Code: God, Family, Household, Career, Personal, Relationships

Daily To-Do List

Mon	Tues	Wed	Thurs	Fri
Mon	Tues	Wed	Thurs	Fri

1. _____ _____ _____ _____ _____

2. _____ _____ _____ _____ _____

3. _____ _____ _____ _____ _____

4. _____ _____ _____ _____ _____

5. _____ _____ _____ _____ _____

6. _____ _____ _____ _____ _____

My Weekly Meal Plan

Delicious, Nutritious, and No Time at All!

Week of: _____   **Notes (recipe page #s)**

Monday

Breakfast: _____

Lunch: _____

Dinner: _____

Tuesday

Breakfast: _____

Lunch: _____

Dinner: _____

Wednesday

Breakfast: _____

Lunch: _____

Dinner: _____

Thursday

Breakfast: _____

Lunch: _____

Dinner: _____

Friday

Breakfast: _____

Lunch: _____

Dinner: _____

Saturday: _____

Sunday: _____

Grocery List

Produce	Canned/ Packaged	Dairy
_____	_____	_____
_____	_____	_____
_____	_____	_____
_____	_____	_____
_____	_____	_____
_____	_____	_____
_____	_____	_____
_____	_____	_____
_____	_____	_____
_____	_____	_____
_____	_____	_____
_____	_____	_____
_____	_____	_____
_____	_____	_____
_____	_____	_____
_____	_____	_____
_____	_____	_____
_____	_____	_____
_____	_____	_____

Grocery List

Meats	Freezer	Other
_____	_____	_____
_____	_____	_____
_____	_____	_____
_____	_____	_____
_____	_____	_____
_____	_____	_____
_____	_____	_____
_____	_____	_____
_____	_____	_____
_____	_____	_____
_____	_____	_____
_____	_____	_____
_____	_____	_____
_____	_____	_____
_____	_____	_____
_____	_____	_____
_____	_____	_____
_____	_____	_____
_____	_____	_____
_____	_____	_____
_____	_____	_____

Review my Month

What did I do well?

_____

_____

_____

_____

What can I improve for next month?

_____

_____

_____

_____

Now, plan your next month!

How to Renew Your Spirit

Renew, as defined by the *Webster Dictionary*, means *"to make new or nearly new by restoring."* I don't know about you, but I don't want to spend my life feeling burnt out, panicked and over-stressed. I want to feel restored and renewed.

Just like our physical bodies, in order to stay alive, our spirits must eat spiritual food. Being in the presence of God, feeds my spirit. Simply put, daily renewal is being with God. Jesus is *"the bread of life"* (John 6:35). In our fast paced, noisy and technology driven world, we desperately need space to renew our spirits.

For me, renewal often looks like resting on my bed and seeking God. The best part is that when you call out to God, He promises that *"[He] will answer you and tell you great and mighty things. . ."* (Jer. 33:3). When I seek God, I feel peace, love and rest. It's being in His presence that brings me life. Sometimes, He shares secrets and other times He whispers a scripture for me to read. It's our secret place — a place where I share my heart, and He shares His heart. He longs to have a secret place with every person, including you.

At other times, renewal looks like, what I call, a PB&J sandwich.

☼ Prayer/Praise (talking, listening, and being grateful).

☼ Bible (reading God's written word).

✪ Journal (writing what I hear directly from God or what's on my heart).

Since this is a relationship with the Living God, there is no formula for renewal. It simply starts with a relationship with Jesus. When I was only five, I realized that I had a problem. My problem was that my heart wasn't perfect, holy or worthy to be in the presence of my perfect Creator. Romans 3:23 (NAS) described my heart condition very well. *"For all have sinned and fall short of the glory of God."* Thank goodness, I found my solution. It was Jesus.

Approximately 2000 years ago, Jesus, God's only perfect Son, died on a cross to pay for my mistakes, so that if I believe and receive Him, I might have life or spiritual connection with God. Jesus said to him, ***"I am the way, the truth, and the life; no one comes to the Father, but through me"*** (John 14:6). So quietly and by myself, I thanked Jesus for dying for my mistakes and asked Him to come into my heart. He paid for my access to re-connect with the living, loving Father God and He also sent His Holy Spirit to live inside of me to be my comforter and teacher. That started my relationship with the living God. Soon after, He began to show up in very real and wonderful ways.

I'm having a great time getting to know God and I'm thankful that Jesus made that possible. Now, I grow that relationship and I renew my spirit, by *"[seeking]*, first, His kingdom ..."* (Matt 6:33) in our secret place. Your relationship with God begins when you believe and receive Jesus' payment for your mistakes as well. You can quietly tell Jesus, just like I did. But it doesn't stop there. Now, you can make space each day to seek God and His kingdom and renew your spirit with His presence, peace, faith, hope and love. He'll take you on an incredible heart journey.

ENDNOTES

1 Flylady.net

2 Osteen, Victoria. *Love Your Life: Living Happy, Healthy, and Whole.* New York: Free, 2008. 89.

3 Wilder, Laura Ingalls. *Little House in the Big Woods.* [S.l.]: Harpercollins, 2008. 29.

4 Dellutri, Laura. *Speed Cleaning 101.* Des Moines, Iowa: Meredith Books, 2005. 66-67.

5 Leaf, Caroline. *The Gift in You.* Southlake, Tex.: Inprov, 2009.

CONTACT ME

For continued support and ideas, for scheduling a workshop
near you, or to order books:

Go to Http://totalhomemakeover.com
Contact Renee Metzler
E-mail: nrmetzler@windstream.net
Mail: Renee Metzler
165 Main Street
Turbotville, PA 17772

For more information about
AMBASSADOR INTERNATIONAL
please visit:

www.ambassador-international.com
@AmbassadorIntl
www.facebook.com/AmbassadorIntl